4·28·71

Great Ideas in MUSIC

Great Ideas in MUSIC

PERCY M. YOUNG

DAVID WHITE COMPANY - NEW YORK

1586641

CONTENTS

PREFACE

TO ASK a composer how he composes is apt to be an
embarrassment to him. More often than not he doesn't
know, or doesn't particularly want to know. How does one
swim, or run, or make strokes at tennis? If one does these things
at all well one does them, as we say, naturally. To a composer
the act of composition is natural.

However, although one is inclined to a particular activity there
are techniques to be learned. At this point we begin to see that
no one works, or plays, quite alone. One depends on others – for
training, for advice, and for encouragement. And if equipment is
needed it must be supplied.

Whenever something is done it is the result of co-operation, of
many people working together. It is the sum total of many
different ideas.

Sometimes a composer is pictured as an isolated person, aloof
from society, and content to compose as and when he is moved
to do so. That picture belongs to fiction and not to fact.

The true composer is at all times aware of what has gone on
in his own field, and of what is going on. He keeps an ear open
for new combinations of sounds in the compositions of other
people. He studies and discusses theories, both old and new,
concerning the structure and purpose of music. He keeps an eye
on improvements to instruments and the invention of new
instruments. He makes himself aware of progress in performing
techniques.

Now where is the individuality of the composer in all this?
Before he starts a composer has an *idea* of the work he is going

to write. He sees the shape in his mind's eye, knows more or less what resources he will need, determines the purpose and length of the composition to be – and so on. In this process he is, often unconsciously, considering ideas from many sources. In the end these become part of his own. Thus every piece of music that is worth anything at all is the outward shape of an individual idea.

In the course of musical history there have been major turning-points. From time to time an idea has been put forth and the whole character of music has been altered. In this book I set out some of these turning-points. Some of them concern the character of instruments, or even parts of the mechanism of instruments; some concern the nature and theory of music; some relate to music and its connection with the other arts. Taken together they provide some kind of answer to the question : what is music? I also believe that they make it unnecessary to ask the question contained in the first sentence of this Preface.

In order clearly to explain some points examples in music type are given. It is intended that these should be played on the piano (and/or sung). Music only comes to life when it is heard. At the end of the book a list of recordings emphasises this point. It is hoped that the reader will listen to the music proposed and that he will add to the given list by noting recordings of other works noticed in the text. There are also given a number of recommended, authoritative books, which, if not immediately to be read from cover to cover, are to be referred to.

Having read the book, heard the recordings, and consulted the relevant literature, the reader may very well find that he has developed ideas of his own. If one of these may one day be described as a 'great idea' then the writing of this book will have been worth while.

For permission to quote from copyright works the author is indebted to Universal Edition (London) Ltd. (p. 19), the Dreililien-Verlag (Richard Birnbach), Berlin 45 (p. 20), and Jean Jobert, Paris (p. 110).

P.M.Y.

Great Ideas in MUSIC

I
The Beginning of "Modern" Music

ONE has to begin somewhere. It is helpful to start with something familiar. If you sit down at the piano (if you can play the piano) you will be able to play the notes shown above. You may even recognise what is called the 'chromatic' scale: a row of notes each a half- or semi-tone distant from its neighbour. There are twelve notes shown above. When we have played them we can start with the same sequence all over again, but an octave (eight notes) higher, and then again – and again. . . .

How can music be made from these twelve notes? That is what the music of today is about. The composer looks at, or

rather listens to, these twelve notes and says to himself, 'Where
do we go from here?"

Fifty years ago most people thought that they knew what
music was. Maybe it was difficult to describe in words, but the
general principles underlying all the familiar kinds of music
were felt to be firmly established. If the word melody was used
it suggested one way in which sounds could behave. So too with
other terms, such as harmony, rhythm, instrumentation. These
terms seemed important. There was another which at that time
seemed even more important to music students. That was 'form'
– which is still a kind of 'sacred cow' in some places where music
is taught.

Young men (and a few young women) who hoped to become
composers went to teachers – often to excellent teachers – who
showed them how to write melodies, how to add harmonies, or
chords, to these melodies, how to distribute sounds among voices
or instruments, how to spread melodies across pages of manuscript paper so that some orderly pattern, or form, appeared.
The student tried to do as he was told. His music began to
resemble that of other composers who had for centuries observed
the same basic principles.

The strongest principle was that of tonality. Music, it seemed,
was divinely ordained to belong to two systems of tonality. The
one was called the *major*, the other the *minor*. It is likely that if
you play the piano, or sing in a school choir, or learn 'theory'
as it is called, you will still hear a good deal about the major
and minor scales. You will read about them in more detail in
Chapter 6.

But today to the majority of younger composers, in the
Western world at least, the old tyranny – as it seemed – of the
major–minor tonal system of which the scales we learn to play
on the piano were emblems, is past.

That this is so is almost entirely due to one man, the Austrian
composer, theorist, and teacher Arnold Schoenberg (1874–1951).

Schoenberg is almost the only man at any time to have appeared to revolutionise Western music single-handed. Before Schoenberg one set of notions concerning the structure of musical compositions prevailed. After Schoenberg we find a new set of notions. In general most music-lovers would claim to be able to understand the music that they hear that was composed up to the end of the nineteenth century. With regard to music of the twentieth century in general many would have doubts. So far as the music of the 1960s is listened to at all by the ordinary run of concert-goers few claims would be made to understand it. At this point we should stop and ask ourselves what we mean by 'understanding' music. It is hard to find an answer, but this book sets out to show how an answer might be found. It will not, however, be the same answer for everybody.

That people say they do not understand 'modern music' is not solely due to Schoenberg. But he encouraged young musicians to believe in themselves and in the long run gave them a new kind of confidence. The enterprising modern composer does not sit down with a set of rule-books to find out how to compose. He goes about seeking out new sounds, new patterns of sounds, and sets them out in what seems to him the most effective way. That means that in the end there is no body of music that we can easily recognise by common features which enable us to refer to it intelligently as 'modern music'. There are many different kinds of modern music.

The reason for this lies in a statement by Schoenberg. He wrote in 1933 that a composer should not think of a style and then try to make his musical idea fit the style, but that he should try to make the style – the method of setting out, that is – grow naturally out of the idea. Those were not Schoenberg's exact words, but that is what he meant. What he was saying was what the greater composers of the past had, in fact, done. But it needed re-saying.

It is important to realise that all the composers we now count as great will even now seem to be 'modern' in many ways. It was, for instance, Joseph Haydn who said: 'What is the good of such rules [of composition]? Art is free and should not be hindered by mechanical regulations. The experienced ear is the only guide –' And what he had to say about the 'idea' of a piece of music may be compared with what Schoenberg wrote: 'If an idea seemed good to me, and satisfactory to the ear and to the emotions, I would soon excuse small mistakes in musical grammar than give up something that to me was beautiful. . . .'

But the 'public', even the general body of musical enthusiasts, tends to be a hard taskmaster.

How hard is shown by the life of Schoenberg.

At the time of Schoenberg's birth Vienna, made famous by Mozart and Haydn, by Beethoven and Schubert, by Brahms, by Mahler and Bruckner, was virtually the musical capital of the world. It was the city in which the symphony was brought to its peak, and in which the techniques of orchestral playing were brought to near perfection by the Vienna Philharmonic Orchestra. The atmosphere of the city was such that it was hard to escape from the influence of music.

Like many other small boys, Schoenberg, the son of a shopkeeper, learned the violin, and at an early age began to compose violin duets which he played with his teacher. The death of his father made it difficult for Schoenberg to continue his studies as he would have wished. As a young man he worked for a time in a bank. But his absorption in the creative aspects of music, stimulated by his love of the music of Brahms and Wagner, urged him to continue to compose. He played chamber music; he discussed poetry and philosophy with one friend and mathematics and the theory of music with another. And he was much interested in painting.

Chamber music – that is music for a small group of musicians – teaches us to concentrate on the essentials of music. The most important details of design are shown clearly, while in comparison with orchestral music, say, variety of tone and of expression is limited. In listening to a string trio, or quartet, for instance, we can be aware of every single note and we can follow each instrumental line as it goes on its way. Chamber music therefore demands concentration – whether from composer, player, or listener. Schoenberg's interest in this form of music was connected with his interests in philosophy, and mathematics, and painting, and poetry.

One of the difficulties facing a young composer is having his music performed. Schoenberg had some lessons from Alexander von Zemlinsky, a composer and conductor. Zemlinsky (whose sister became Schoenberg's wife) arranged for a string quartet by Schoenberg to be played at a musical-society concert in 1898. In the next year or two he composed songs and a string sextet (a work for six instruments). The songs were said to have been similar to those of Hugo Wolf, another famous Viennese composer, while the string sextet used harmonies in a way that reminds the listener of the methods of Wagner. The sextet carried the title *Verklärte Nacht (Transfigured Night)*. The work was inspired by a poem by Richard Dehmel and because it tries to capture the spirit of the poem it belongs to that class of music described as 'programme music'. *Verklärte Nacht*, the beauty of the sounds of which is to be appreciated even by those who are suspicious of 'modern music', may now be heard not only in its original form but also in the version later made for string orchestra by the composer.

The early songs and *Verklärte Nacht* were recognised as skilful creations; but because certain chords were used in unfamiliar ways there were those who, relying on the rule-book, condemned the composer. He, however, was undeterred and went on to explore all kinds of further possibilities in music.

One of the difficulties of being a composer is that one tends to find that everything seems already to have been composed!

In fact, of course, this is not really the case because the possibilities of arranging sounds are limitless. They are not, however, limitless if you stay within a system that other people have exploited pretty fully.

At the beginning of his career Schoenberg did what all other young composers try to do. He put himself among the composers of the day by writing works which he hoped the public would find readily intelligible. He admired the music of Johannes Brahms and Richard Wagner, composers who had also had to fight against prejudice and misunderstanding, but he looked at their music without preconceived ideas. In the music of Brahms he recognised a new flexibility of rhythm and metre; new ways of using harmonies; and a sense of musical logic that showed how the 'idea' could generate its proper form. In later life, in 1937, Schoenberg showed his particular interest in the musical thought of Brahms by making an orchestral arrangement of Brahms' Pianoforte Quintet in G minor (Op. 25).

Wagner was one of the greatest masters of opera who ever lived. In transforming human behaviour into terms of music (we shall come to this in Chapter 12) he expanded the vocabulary of music to such an extent that he seemed almost to have made a new vocabulary.

Wagner broke down the barriers that had seemed to exist between tonalities, and in his later works it no longer made much sense to refer to 'key', since one merged into another. In this connection you may turn to page 183. If this was so effective, then what was the point of retaining the old scheme of tonality which, nevertheless, had served composers well during the eighteenth and nineteenth centuries?

The traditional view of music is that it 'developed'; that after A came B, and after B came C, and so on. All the while music was subtly changing, but since the change was gradual it was not particularly disturbing. At best this view represents a half-truth. But even a half-truth is to be taken notice of. Schoenberg certainly believed up to a point that if one went on working in some field of music well cultivated by some admired composer something worthwhile would eventually emerge. So he composed a great work using all the resources of voice and orchestra that Wagner had used. This was a setting of poems by the Danish poet, Jens Peter Jacobsen (1847–85). These poems told the love-story of King Waldemar I of Denmark – which was set in the castle of Gurre.

In order to write down his music Schoenberg needed special manuscript paper – with forty-eight staves to a page. The composer who asked for everything that the *Gurre-Lieder* (*Songs of Gurre*) requires in the way of instruments was asking for trouble! The larger the orchestra, the greater the expense of performance. And relatively unknown composers are rarely likely to be looked on with favour by concert promoters if their demands appear exorbitant.

It is not surprising that although Schoenberg began to compose the *Gurre-Lieder* in 1900 it was not until thirteen years later that it received its first performance. This took place in Vienna on February 23, 1913. To say that the audience did not like the music is an understatement. People shouted. Free fights broke out. Women fainted. One man subsequently brought a legal action for assault against another, who had disagreed with his views on Schoenberg. Now this is less a reflection on this particular musical work than of the intensity of the feeling for music of the Viennese of that time. Today we see what can happen when intense emotions are aroused among the supporters, and perhaps the opponents, of pop groups. But violent demonstrations about 'serious' music are less likely. This shows that the general attitude to music has changed somewhat in fifty years.

What the conservative music-lovers of Vienna feared was that music, as they knew it, was being destroyed. Up to a point, of course, they were right; for any change means that something has been destroyed or put aside. What they did not understand was that the world as they knew it was about to be destroyed. A little over a year after the first performance of *Gurre-Lieder* war broke out, at the end of which the Austrian Empire was no more.

An idea is the result of conflict. The artist (in this case) argues with himself as he sets the new against the old and weighs its merits. He may also argue with the society in which he lives, and even suffer persecution. To many people new ideas seem dangerous. Schoenberg experienced opposition at every level.

When he had begun the composition of *Gurre-Lieder* he obtained a modest post as a theatre musician in Berlin. He conducted music-hall entertainments and operettas. The one song he composed for the theatre in Berlin was performed only once, because everybody said it was too difficult. In 1903 he returned to Vienna. There he began to establish himself as a teacher and also as a composer. Among the first pupils of Schoenberg were two young composers who were to appear also as key figures in the development of twentieth century music: they were Alban Berg (1865–1935) and Anton Webern (1883–1945).

In his earlier works Schoenberg, as we have seen, showed musical kinship with Wagner. But all the time he was asking himself what was the purpose that lay behind music. The elements that attracted him in Wagner's works were unity of design (how Wagner achieved this is described in Chapter 12); the way in which tonal conventions were overthrown; and the masterly manner in which themes were united in *counterpoint* – where one theme sounds against another, or others. The great master of counterpoint – who inspired Wagner – was Johann Sebastian Bach; and Bach's masterpieces were models of economy. A fugue by Bach deals with one, relatively simple, musical idea, as is shown in more detail in Chapter 6. Schoenberg also made arrangements of works by Bach.

The way towards simplicity is the way towards truth. It

seemed to many – in literature, drama, and painting, as well as in music – that all the complexities of Romantic art had led away from truth. Insofar as music was concerned there was a great deal that appeared to have been written to attract the listener into a kind of never-never-land: it is not difficult to recall pieces of this kind, some of which still retain their ability to enable us to 'escape'. Perhaps this is what some people want. But the composer who thinks about his work is reluctant to believe that music is no more important than this.

Both in *Verklärte Nacht* and *Gurre-Lieder* Schoenberg showed the power of contrapuntal design, but still within sight of the familiar behaviour of contrasting melodies within a settled harmonic framework. The next step was to release melody, and contrapuntal combinations of melodies, from the control of the chord. There was no particular reason why melodies should have surrendered their freedom to the chordal system as they often seemed to have done in the nineteenth century. But complete freedom from all discipline leads to disorder; and the artist above all searches for order and unity. In his debate with himself Schoenberg asked why melody, harmony, and counterpoint should each be thought of separately. Why could they not all be seen as different aspects of a single idea?

Schoenberg moved steadily towards this ideal. In his songs he set the voice new tasks, for he created unusual patterns

Ex.2   Voice line *(words omitted)*   (Six Orchestral Songs, Op. 8)

(though this also had been anticipated by Wagner). (Ex. 2). You will realise that you need to *think* before you sing this voice line, simply because it is not like other singing patterns to which you may be accustomed.

In the Quartet in D minor the opening looks like this (Ex. 3).

There are three separate melodic lines, each of which develops its own material. In the course of the quartet these themes reappear many times, but in different and fascinating combinations: sometimes one is uppermost, sometimes another. This shows the treatment of a limited amount of musical material. But the music appears to grow, developing from within itself rather than seeking for new material from outside. If you now turn to page 86 you will see how similar Schoenberg's lay-out is to that of Bach, and in this way appreciate how strong Bach's influence has been in the twentieth century.

Schoenberg was fortunate in that a famous string quartet, led by Arnold Rosé, a teacher at the Vienna State Academy of Music, championed his cause. When the Rosé Quartet performed the D minor quartet and its successor, in F sharp minor, there was an unfriendly demonstration on the part of the audience. Perhaps they felt cheated because the composer had condensed the usual four movements into one continuous movement. A similar demonstration took place when the *Chamber Symphony* was performed in 1909. In comparison with previous symphonies this was concise and it was also continuous. Here may be noticed the coming together of melody and harmony (Ex. 4). The group of melody notes here makes a new kind of chord. This symphony departs from the idea of symphony as a work for 'full orchestra'. It was originally written (although rescored later in Schoenberg's

life for larger orchestra) for fifteen instruments, each of which was thought of as an independent voice in the music.

While he was reducing the bulk of music in this way Schoenberg was paying more and more attention to the *quality* of sounds. Hence he exploited instruments in ensembles as soloists, and in his piano pieces departed from all the patterns generally described as 'pianistic' in order to try new sound-groupings, or *sonorities*. Tonality, less and less important, was left behind after the second string quartet, the last work which Schoenberg prefaced with a 'key signature', had been composed.

An important work (well-known, and even popular) of the years preceding the First World War, was *Pierrot Lunaire*, based on twenty-one poems, translated into German, by the French poet Albert Giraud. In this work the words were not to be sung, but declaimed (to approximate pitches shown in the score) against a small group of instruments. In each piece there is a different combination of instruments. In different movements the instruments show treatments of material according to older contrapuntal principles. The eighth movement ('Night') for instance is a *passacaglia* (variations on a recurring bass motiv as shown on page 96), while in the eighteenth we find two *canons* – between piccolo and clarinet, and violin and 'cello – which are reversed; that is to say, with the last note becoming the first and working towards the former first note which is now the last !

'If this is music,' wrote a critic in Berlin after the first performance, on October 16, 1912, 'then I pray that I may not hear it again.'

New sounds; new patterns of sounds; new methods (though based on some which had largely been forgotten) of bringing patterns together: above all a new sense of discord. Fifty years ago most of those who listened to the music of Schoenberg tried to find what was not there – a re-affirmation of what they wanted to find.

If you try to watch a baseball match while all the time comparing it with tennis, or cricket, you will not make much out of it. If, on the other hand, you try to start with a mind free from prejudice and avoid making nonsensical comparisons you will find yourself before long coming to terms with what is going on. So it is with unfamiliar happenings in music.

'That music', you may feel inclined to say, 'is all discord.' That kind of statement is never quite true; for discord is always relative. This we understand now. For while much contemporary music has more and sharper-edged discords freely used than was the case fifty years ago we have grown accustomed to their use and are no longer inclined to question them.

No creative musician works in a vacuum. He may not consciously try to reflect the 'spirit' of the time in which he lives, but in one way or another it is inevitable that he will do so. On the eve of the First World War Schoenberg, encouraged by performances of works in London and Amsterdam, was seen to be a notable, if controversial, figure. One result of the war was to further disrupt all the artistic principles that had previously been regarded as binding. Poets and painters, appalled at the behaviour of which so-called civilised men were capable, tried to find ways and means of looking deeper into the human situation. Very often they moved under the influence of the great Viennese pioneer of psychological analysis, Sigmund Freud. It was imperative to develop new techniques.

One of the most important painters contemporary with

Schoenberg was the Russian-born Wassily Kandinsky (1866–1944). Kandinsky, like Schoenberg, took apart the elements of his art and re-examined their functions. By so doing he developed a style that seemed unrelated to the conventions of realism. Most of his paintings were not narrative, nor descriptive of objects, but abstract. 'If he laboured to study scientifically the mechanics of painting', said one writer, 'and to rediscover quasi-mathematical laws for the use and meaning of colour, it was because . . . he counted on finding in this way meanings which had been unknown till then. The stricter his technique became the more his imagination freed itself.'

This brings us to an all-important point. The artist can only use his art imaginatively – and thus open up new horizons for the rest of us – when he knows precisely what he is doing with his material. The great artist subjects himself to a stern discipline. In the case of the greatest we are aware of this; but we can forget the discipline as we listen to, read, or look at the final work.

Kandinsky was a great teacher. So too was Schoenberg. For a year or two after the First World War, during which his opportunities to compose were limited, this was his main activity. Until 1924 he remained in Vienna, where many young musicians clustered round him. From 1924 until 1935 he taught in Berlin. In the latter year he was dismissed from his teaching post by the Minister of Education : the ideas that Schoenberg was spreading were described as 'unhealthy'; and he was a Jew.

It was during this decade that the idea for which Schoenberg is most famous was shaped into a principle on which other composers could work. Like all important ideas this one was basically very simple.

As you can easily discover at the piano an octave – taking in all the white and black keys – consists of twelve equal semitones (see Ex. 1). As we play them all are of equal importance. If, however, we repeat one note that then assumes a greater importance – because it becomes more memorable. Tonal music depends

on one note, together with its 'natural' harmonies, acting as
guide and leader. We speak, for instance, of the key of D major,
meaning that D is the central feature of the melodic and
harmonic design. Schoenberg (and not Schoenberg alone) had
long realised that this attitude to a 'key-note' was limiting : the
composer had always to be thinking of returning to it. *And there
was no good artistic reason why he should.* Let us, said Schoenberg, develop the independence of each of the twelve sounds.

In 1923 he composed *Five Piano Pieces* (Op. 23) and in the
last of these he showed the principle of a twelve-note (or twelve-
tone) principle. This principle was carried into his *Serenade*
(Op. 24), for clarinet, bass clarinet, mandolin, guitar, viola,
'cello, and bass voice. By the time the *Suite* for piano (Op. 25)
and the Wind Quintet (Op. 26) were issued in 1924 the nature
of the new principle was clear.

The foundation of the technique is an arrangement of the
twelve basic sounds within the octave, as shown at the head of
the chapter. The composer is free to arrange these sounds as he
will. Therefore in the Wind Quintet Schoenberg used this
thematic 'tone-row' (Ex. 5). Note that while all these note-names

may be found *within* the compass of an octave the composer is
permitted to go outside this limit, in order, of course, to suit the
character of various instruments.

The device to be found most often in music is variation of
thematic matter. Schoenberg pursued the practice of variation
rigorously. For by concentrating on one musical idea, of which
various aspects may be shown by variation, unity is achieved.
The tone-row shown above may be varied by inverting it, that
is by reversing the intervals. Where the theme went down, it now
goes up, and vice versa (Ex. 6). The original row of notes may

Ex. 6

also be turned back to front. And so may the inversion. Either or both may be transposed. That is, a start may be made at a higher or lower pitch and the interval relationships maintained at the new pitch.

The note-row is developed melodically. When there is a group of instruments involved (as in the case of the five belonging to the wind quintet) it is developed contrapuntally. But the notes of a row may also be used chordally, as shown on page 21.

Of the works in this idiom one of the most celebrated was Schoenberg's *Variations for Orchestra* (Op. 31) in which every detail of the method is carefully worked out. Yet here, as in the *Violin Concerto*, the method is less important than the result of its application.

The twelve-tone technique is not difficult to use. This is one of its attractions to the young composer. It also leaves a great deal of room for the inventive talent of the musician. The 'rules' can be much less severe than those which were finally evolved with the tonal scheme. (Some of Schoenberg's disciples have made the principle *look* complicated; but that was not his fault.) Above all, adherence to the principle shows a whole new vocabulary of sound combinations. This vocabulary is enlarged by the availability of new sonorities (combination of instruments, spacing of sounds, etc.).

After his dismissal from Berlin, Schoenberg, like many other European artists and scholars, emigrated to the United States. Until his death he taught in the University of California. In his later years Schoenberg modified his system to some extent, accepting that it could be associated with other, even tonal, concepts. In a masterly work, *Variations on a Recitative*, for organ, the composer's skill in using the resources of variation form as expressive of the particular and unique qualities of the instrument is remarkable. There is not a great literature of organ music outside the works of Bach. Schoenberg has composed one of the few great works within this literature.

In this work one is made aware how much what we call expression depends on a true understanding of what a particular instrument (or group of instruments) is capable of.

In his late years Schoenberg composed music which met other music of the period, of different styles, in being directly related to the problems of the age. In his setting of Byron's *Ode to Napoleon* (New York Philharmonic Symphony Orchestra concert, 1944) Schoenberg spoke out in moving terms against tyranny and in praise of the vision of George Washington. In *A Survivor from Warsaw* (Boston Symphony Orchestra concert, 1948), where also a narrator is used and the idea of *Sprechstimme* further developed, the composer comments on the horrors of the concentration camp. In these works the technique as such takes a back place : what overwhelms the listener is the force of this music to achieve this effect.

Schoenberg had the courage to dismantle the accepted techniques of music. He then looked at what lay about him and began to build up afresh, in a manner acceptable to the modern mind. He pared away what was not essential. In so doing he enabled many to see how to set about musical composition in such a way that invention would have its greatest scope. It is not possible to hear modern music without being aware of the debt that is owed to Schoenberg. Among those who have learned how to apply his ideas, though without slavishly following them, are Anton Webern, Alban Berg, Nikos Skalkottas, Luigi Nono, Luigi Dallapiccola, Humphrey Searle, Wolfgang Fortner, and Roberto Gerhard, while the impact of the Schoenbergian idea may be noticed even in the works of such older composers as Stravinsky and Bartók.

A great reformer is the one who codifies an idea of reformation that is being sought by many. Thus although Schoenberg sometimes seems to be an isolated figure, as time passes we see him as within a main stream of musical and philosophic thought. In the end we find that he does express something that needs to be expressed.

Once it was the abstract quality of Schoenberg's art that impressed people. Since the famous Covent Garden production of his opera *Moses and Aaron* in 1965 it has become clear that Schoenberg's greatest music is concerned with emotion as well as intellect.

The sculptor Henry Moore once wrote of his own art – which is almost as 'abstract' as music – in a manner which helps us towards an understanding of modern music, particularly that of Schoenberg:

> 'Abstract qualities of design are essential to the value of a work, but to me of equal importance is the psychological human element. If both abstract and human elements are welded together in a work, it must have a fuller, deeper meaning.'

This shows us however much an artist tries to develop new techniques he cannot make technique an end in itself. In listening to the music of today then you should not try to think about *how* a work is composed until you feel that you know *why* it has been composed. The answer to this is not to be found in a rule-book, but only in the way in which you feel that the work makes you want to listen to it, twice, or three times, and not merely once. Many people listen to music with only half-an-ear. What Schoenberg suggested was that we should listen with both ears.

II
The Pianoforte

IF ONE had to choose one invention that had had the greatest influence on the history of music until the coming of gramophone, radio, and tape-recorder, it might very well be that of the piano. That would be because through playing the piano more people have gained insight into the broader nature of music than in any other way. Think of all those you know who have some musical talent. Most of them will be able to play the piano, even if they are singers or violinists.

Let us see what sort of things the piano is capable of. It reproduces rhythmic effects. It has a 'striking' power, and is, therefore, percussive. Its rhythmic and percussive character is

exploited in jazz – and in other departments of modern music.
It can show the full range of harmony, and the piano music we
know best is often characterised by passages of chords. But music
which depends on the interplay of melodic lines that run along
against one another as in the *Inventions* and *Fugues* of Bach
can be shown with great clarity, so that one may, if one wishes,
follow the progress of any one of the lines. Because of its large
compass – the keyboard covers more than seven octaves – there
is a wealth of contrast between high sounds and low sounds. This
was appreciated by Schoenberg in his piano pieces.

Sometimes you will notice in a piece that a passage is marked
cantabile – in a singing manner. Much of the beauty of the
instrument comes from the particular singing quality that it can
give. The name of the instrument suggests the quality which first
commended it : *piano* = soft; *forte* = loud. The pianoforte
came in answer to the need to make a keyboard instrument that
was sensitive, widely ranging, but subtle in expression. The first
notable makers of pianos lived in a period when composers were
trying to give greater expressive power to music of all kinds, that
is in the eighteenth century. In many ways (if we leave aside our
own day) the eighteenth century is the most interesting in the
history of music, for so many vital changes then took place.

We discover then, that the piano, the most familiar and
universal of instruments, has a history of little more than two
hundred years.

How is tone produced from a piano?

The player presses down an ivory-covered 'key'. The 'key'
then sets in motion a delicate and complicated set of levers,
which in turn move a felt-covered hammer upwards to strike
against a 'string', or wire, with many such strings stretched across
a metal frame. The string being set in motion generates a
particular sound, of which the pitch depends on the length and
tension of the string. The sound is carried because of the wooden
sound-board that in a grand piano lies below, or in the case of

an upright piano behind the string. The sound-board amplifies the sounds in the same way as the 'belly' of a stringed instrument. Above the string there is a 'damper', also felt-covered. When the key is at rest the damper lies against the string. When the key is pressed down the damper is moved away from the string, returning to its resting position when the key is released by the player. This action of the damper prevents further vibration of the string and the sound ceases. The following diagram shows how this apparatus works in respect of a single string.

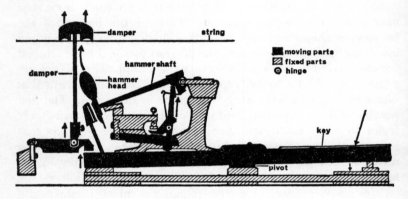

(Diagram 1)

The piano possesses an almost infinite variety of tone. As we have seen, a hammer strikes a string and a sound is produced. But this is only the beginning.

If you look at the inside of a piano you will notice that the lowest, or *bass*, notes (on the left hand side of the instrument) come from single strings round which are wrapped lengths of copper coiling. This gives a richer tone than a naked string. The low sounds that we hear are, however, not quite so simple as they seem. For they also contain certain higher sounds which, although we may not be able to distinguish them separately except by carefully training the ear, enrich the basic, or fundamental sound. These upper sounds are termed *harmonics*, and you may read more about them in Chapter 4. When the pitch of a harmonic coincides with the pitch of one of the upper strings it also sets that string vibrating in sympathy.

If you move up the keyboard and press down one of the middle keys you will see that the hammer hits not one string but two. These, tuned to the same pitch, reinforce each other. The reason for having two strings is that the higher the sound the weaker it is in harmonics. Two strings help to intensify the harmonics. At the top, or extreme *treble*, end, three strings will be seen. These very high sounds, almost entirely lacking in harmonic colouring, are dry and brittle.

When a hammer travels fast the resulting sound is loud, whereas when it travels slowly the sound is soft. To control the speed of the action the player must be careful to calculate the weight he applies to the keyboard. This is a most important factor in determining the quality of tone.

If you look at the piano again you will see two pedals – one for each foot. If you press that on your left and hold it down and then sound a note you will notice that the sound continues for quite a long time. This left-side pedal is called the sustaining pedal. By its careful use we may increase the singing quality of the tone. What happens is that the dampers are prevented from returning to their normal resting position with the result that the strings continue to vibrate.

The other pedal will give a softer, more veiled, tone. When it is operated the hammers are moved to such a position that instead of striking the two or three strings they only strike one. Other mechanisms have been used to give a softer tone. Sometimes the hammers were moved nearer to the strings so that by travelling a shorter distance they necessarily gave a gentler tone. Sometimes in the past the pedal moved a piece of felt between hammers and strings. This method altered the tone so drastically that it was discontinued.

We begin to see that the pianist is in control of a very complex and delicate machine, which leaves a good deal of room for error. A simple jab of the finger that is not meant can suddenly give an unexpected loudness and hardness that can wreck a gentle phrase. By keeping the sustaining pedal down fractionally too long sounds which should be heard separately and distinctly simply form into a kind of musical fog. There are, of course, many other opportunities of making errors. The simplest and most familiar error is to 'play a wrong note'.

But playing a wrong note is less of a crime than playing the right note in the wrong way. By doing the latter the player is denying the character of the instrument. A great performer realises that his instrument has its own personality and makes sure that this personality is appreciated by his listeners. We often speak of the personality of such a pianist as Sviatoslav Richter or John Ogdon : what we really mean is that they have the genius to understand and to demonstrate the personality of their instrument.

The personality of the instrument is also the inspiration of the composer. The great composers of music for the piano knew how to bring out many aspects of personality. This you will discover if you listen to the piano music of Mozart, Beethoven, John Field, Chopin, Schumann, Brahms, Debussy, or Hindemith – and, of course, of many other composers.

But the composer would be helpless without the craftsmen who make musical instruments. In the case of the piano we find ourselves back in the eighteenth century, a period in which many manufacturers of musical instruments flourished because such instruments were in great demand.

At the beginning of the eighteenth century the most widely used keyboard instruments (apart from the organ, which operates on quite different principles) were the clavichord and the harpsi-

chord. In each case sound was produced, as in the case of the
piano, by setting strings in vibration. Each of the strings (or
rather pair of strings) of the clavichord was set in motion by
being touched by a small piece of brass – a tangent – operated

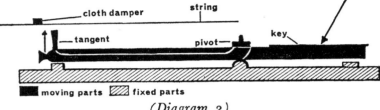

(Diagram 2)

from the keyboard (Diagram 2). The mechanism of the clavichord is simple. The tone is very sensitive and beautiful. But it
is also very small and a clavichord can only properly be appreciated in a small room. Even then one has to listen hard!

The clavichord in shape was oblong. The harpsichord, however, resembled the grand piano, the strings running away from

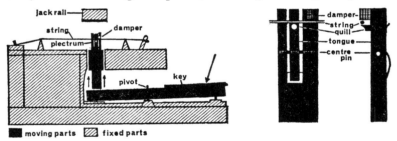

(Diagram 3)

the keyboard in similar manner. The sound of the harpsichord
was produced by a 'plectrum', of quill or more often of leather,
plucking the strings (Diagram 3). The harpsichord was more
complex than the clavichord and frequently had two keyboards,

or manuals, and stops (similar to those found on the organ) which could produce different effects.

Both clavichord and harpsichord may be heard today since there is a renewed interest in music of the so-called Renaissance and the Baroque periods, and the tone-colours used then are a source of inspiration to many adventurous modern composers. Above all the clavichord and the harpsichord were the instruments known and loved by such masters as Purcell, Domenico Scarlatti, Bach, and Handel. King Henry VIII of England played the harpsichord, so did his daughter Elizabeth I, and so, nearly two hundred years later, did Frederick the Great, King of Prussia. That gives some idea of the long period during which the harpsichord reigned supreme.

Frederick the Great was anxious to make Prussia an important influence in Europe. One way of doing this was to build a powerful army. This he did. Another was to educate people. This he did too. Education, however, depends on a free flow of new ideas. A student of philosophy (as it was thus understood) Frederick entertained the greatest philosopher in Europe, the Frenchman Voltaire, for whose ideas he was grateful. But Frederick knew that there were many different kinds of ideas, and some belong to music. As a lover of music Frederick, who played the flute and also composed, did many things for which we can be grateful. He insisted that music should be a part of the State system of education. He recognised that a nation's music is an important part of its heritage. He therefore laid great stress on the masterpieces of German music. He built a new Opera House (now the State Opera House in East Berlin), and he entertained John Sebastian Bach as his guest at his palace at Potsdam.

When Bach visited Potsdam the King one day took him into his Music Room and showed him a new instrument: a pianoforte, made by the famous instrument-maker Gottfried Silbermann. It is said that Silbermann had shown his pianos to Bach some years before this visit to Potsdam and that Bach (who loved the clavichord, of the manufacture of which Silbermann was an acknowledged master) had not thought much of them. Perhaps Frederick the Great, who possessed three such instruments, persuaded him to alter his opinion.

Silbermann, however, was not the inventor of the piano section. He followed a principle that was discovered by an Italian manufacturer, Bartolommeo di Francesco Cristofori. Cristofori, maker of harpsichords and clavichords to the Grand Duke of Tuscany, originated the hammer mechanism which is the distinguishing feature of the pianoforte. A long account of Cristofori's invention was published in 1711 by a writer named Scipione Mattei.

'I will say', he wrote, 'that instead of the usual *jacks* that produce sound by quills, there is a row of little hammers that strike the string from below, the tops of which are covered with leather. . . .' Mattei not only praised the invention of Cristofori but also perceived how the character of music could be affected. Observing that in orchestral music in Rome the playing was marked by changes of expression he went on :

'Now, of this diversity and alteration of tone, in which bowed stringed instruments are outstanding, the harpsichord is quite incapable' where as the new instrument shows 'not only the piano and the forte . . . but also the gradations and diversity of power as in a violoncello.' Mattei said that this was the ideal accompaniment to a singer, which shows how forward-looking he was. He also noted that many people objected to the new instrument. This, he added, was due primarily to 'the general want of knowledge of how to play it'.

If the Italians did not do much about the pianoforte in those early days the Germans showed great interest. Mattei's article was translated and published in a number of encyclopædias of music compiled during the first half of the eighteenth century. It is probable that Silbermann worked from the knowledge gained from one of these encyclopædias. In any event his instruments were very similar to those of Cristofori. They were, as Mattei said of the Italian models, sweet-toned. Long years afterwards this was the quality praised by the musician Karl Zelter, the friend both of Goethe and of Mendelssohn.

In the eighteenth century a young man learned a craft by being apprenticed to a master-craftsman. Gottfried Silbermann had many apprentices. Among them was one Johann Christoph Zumpe. When Zumpe was about ready to launch out on his own account Germany was devastated by the Seven Years War. One of the cities worst affected was Dresden where Zumpe lived. He did what many others did. He packed his bags – making sure that he had his tools – and emigrated, to England.

There he was employed by a Swiss instrument-maker named Tschudi. Zumpe modified the action he had learned from Silbermann and it became known as the 'English single action'. He also popularised the square pianoforte (the instrument in those days was called the forte-piano, but we will give it its modern form for the sake of convenience).

The English do not stand in the front rank of musical nations; but in one way or another they have done much good by stealth – as it were. First of all, there was the matter of giving homes and employment to refugees and indeed to foreigners in general. In the eighteenth century Handel was adopted as an Englishman. Soon after his death Bach's youngest son, John Christian, came to settle in London. This was about the time that Zumpe arrived. And it so happens that the first composer and performer to take a deep interest in the pianoforte in England was John Christian Bach. He gave performances on it and also wrote *concertos* for pianoforte and orchestra which were played at popular concerts in London and also in such provincial cities as Leeds. At the same time Zumpe was manufacturing pianofortes as fast as he could. Thus there was a useful combination of instrument-maker and composer.

The popularity of Zumpe's instruments is shown by references in contemporary writing. In the ninth of his *Letters of Yorick and Eliza* Laurence Sterne makes Yorick write : 'I must entreat that you could procure directions from Mr Zumps [printed so !] in what manner I am to tune my pianoforte [also, surprisingly, printed so] as I design it to be my harmonious companion during the voyage.'

The poet Thomas Gray (who supported every 'modern' movement in music) had been looking after the pianoforte of his friend William Mason : 'You will tell me,' he wrote one day in 1767, 'what to do with your *Zumpe*, which has amused me much here. If you would have it sent down, I had better commit it to the Maker, who will tune it and pack it up. Dr Long has b[r]ought the fellow to it. The base [bass] is not quite of a piece with the treble, and the higher notes are somewhat dry and sticky : the rest discourses very eloquent music.'

Another assistant to Tschudi was John Broadwood, a Scotsman. Having married his employer's daughter Broadwood eventually took over his business. Broadwood was ingenious and imaginative. By 1781 he had made the first Broadwood grand piano, and two years later he patented a pedal mechanism. He also gave up the single bridge which in early pianos, as in the harpsichord, carried the strings, and gave a separate bridge to the bass strings. In 1818 the firm of Broadwood sent one of their instruments to Beethoven, in Vienna, as a mark of their esteem, and also as another hint that he would be very welcome in London. This instrument is now preserved in a museum in Budapest, it having passed after Beethoven's death to the Hungarian musician, Franz Liszt.

Yet another famous English firm was that founded by Robert Stodart in 1776. His son William put on the market in 1795 a 'new invented upright grand pianoforte, of the form of a bookcase', which showed how people were now looking for a piece of furniture as well as a musical instrument. One member

of the family, also Robert Stodart, emigrated to America in
1819 and in the next year went into partnership with William
Dubois. The firm of Dubois and Stodart had its premises in
Broadway.

We should now return to another of the many disciples of
Gottfried Silbermann : Johann Andreas Stein (1728–1792). Stein
was born in the town of Heidesheim and became not only a
maker of keyboard instruments but a performer on them. He
built organs and harpsichords and, inspired by his master Silbermann, took a keen interest in the new pianoforte. When he was
about thirty he went to Paris where he built up his reputation.
After a year or two he returned to Germany, setting up a business
in Augsburg, where he also played the organ in one of the
churches.

In the year 1777 Wolfgang Mozart visited Augsburg, where
he met Stein and played on his piano. In the course of a long
letter home Mozart wrote with enthusiasm, both of Stein's
inventiveness and his devotion to his craft. Among many inventions Stein introduced a mechanism for producing sustained tone
and also the 'una corda' effect, both of which are now controlled
by the foot-pedals. This device consisted of levers to be operated by the knees of the player. Mozart found that Stein's
pianos allowed him to play all kinds of melodic passages with
clarity, while sustained chords kept an even tone. He said that
they were the best instruments of their kind that he had played
on.

Stein worked long hours to perfect his instruments and was
never content until he had tested them by playing different
kinds of music on them. His instruments were expensive. He
rarely let one go for less than three hundred florins, which
was about a year's salary for an averagely good musician employed at one of the ducal courts. But, said Mozart, they were
worth it.

Stein's daughter, Maria Anna or 'Nanette' (1769–1833),

played the piano to Mozart when she was a little girl of eight and he commended her highly. Maria Anna also mastered the techniques of instrument manufacture and the principles of business management. In due course she married one of her father's assistants, Johann Andreas Streicher – also an excellent performer – and they set up in business in Vienna. In some of the pianos made by the Streichers which are still to be seen in some of the more important instrument museums of Europe, there are more than two pedals. In addition to the so-called 'soft' and 'loud' pedals there were sometimes added two extra pedals, one of them to control what was described as 'bassoon' tone, the other to bring into operation percussion instruments. These did not last long because the tone of the piano was so comprehensive in itself.

In later life Maria Streicher was on close terms of friendship with Beethoven. She helped him in housekeeping matters and also worried herself about his health.

There was another member of the Stein family whose place in the history of music is greater than is commonly known. This was Friedrich Stein (1784–1809). He was one of the first notable pianists of Vienna, and from the accounts of his playing we realise that at last the style of piano music had grown well away from that of harpsichord music. 'He played some of Beethoven's most difficult pieces', wrote Johann Reichardt, 'and variations of his own composition, full of invention and deep sentiment.' His manner of performance was characterised by 'a rare power, combined with the deepest feeling'. It was towards that good – 'of deepest feeling' – that the early piano manufacturers aimed.

While the piano was thus developing there was a great spread of interest in music all over Europe. As an instrument for the home the piano was unrivalled – most of all because it could suggest so many different ideas and fulfil so many purposes. Some time before 1831 the Englishman, William Crotch,

Professor of Music at Oxford, emphasised this in a lecture which
he gave (on the musical taste of the nation):

> 'Played on the pianoforte, every species of music, both
> vocal and instrumental, ancient and modern, sacred and
> secular, may be more or less enjoyed. The imagination
> readily supplies the absent words of a finale or chorus pre-
> viously heard at the opera or oratorio. The pianoforte seems
> to speak, and the qualities and tones of different instruments
> seem almost distinguishable.'

In addition to those already mentioned famous names in the
history of the pianoforte include those of Erard, Chickering,
Blüthner and Steinway.

Sébastien Erard (1752–1831), born in Strasbourg, son of a
cabinet-maker and pupil of a harpsichord manufacturer in Paris,
achieved fame by being the first in France to make a piano. This
was in 1777. Erard was inspired to attempt this by the flooding
of the French market with English and German instruments.
Sébastian went into partnership with his brother Jean Baptiste
and their success was not to the liking of the other musical
instrument-makers of France. However, they were helped by the
intervention and support of King Louis XVI. The Erards opened
a branch of their business in London. They made various
improvements to the action of the piano and also to that of the
harp, of which they were notable manufacturers. The most
important improvement in piano action made by the Erards
was called the 'double escapement'. This enabled the hammer
to strike the string again, if needed, without first having had to
fall all the way back to its normal point of rest. Towards the
end of his life Joseph Haydn was delighted to be presented with
an Erard pianoforte.

On June 28, 1824, Franz Liszt, then a boy of eleven and the
wonder of Europe, gave a performance at Drury Lane Theatre,
London. The advertisement said that he had 'consented to

display his inimitable powers on the New Grand Piano Forte, invented by Sébastian Erard'. Liszt loved the Erard instrument and in 1846 he had one sent all the way to Constantinople where he was to give a recital.

By 1789 Charles Albrecht of Philadelphia was manufacturing pianos after English designs. Other early makers working in America were John Geib – in Boston and New York, John Isaac Hawkins – in Philadelphia, and Benjamin Crehore – a friend of the leading musical families of Boston.

In 1823 a young American, Jonas Chickering (1798–1853), founded his own manufacturing business. He had worked for a time with James Stewart, a Scotsman, who had himself trained with the London firm of Collard and Collard, and also with Crehore. Chickering experimented further with the metal frame (which could carry a greater tension of the strings) invented by Alpheus Babcock of Boston, and in 1837 made a square piano embodying this principle. In due course he made grand pianos – which consequently were extremely powerful in tone – on the same principle.

By the middle of the nineteenth century the pianoforte was well established and some of the names of makers that are still famous were well known throughout the world. Among those names that of Blüthner ranks very high, on account of the beautiful and distinctively 'singing' quality of tone that a Blüthner piano gives.

The founder of the firm, which had its headquarters in Leipzig, was Julius Blüthner (1824–1910), who opened his business in 1853. Like others connected with the profession of music in the past the great European manufacturers depended to some extent on royal patronage. Blüthner was piano-maker to the King of Saxony. In 1873 he enhanced the quality of the tone of his pianos by adding to each rather weak upper string an extra string tuned an octave higher that was not struck, but that vibrated in sympathy with the one to which it was toned.

This – the principle had been applied in former times to instruments of the lute family – gave extra resonance.

After the revolution of 1848 many Germans emigrated to America. Among them was one Heinrich Steinway, a piano-maker from Brunswick. With him went three of his sons. Together they established themselves in New York and the firm of Steinway and Sons was founded in 1853. The Steinways modified the design of the piano in various ways – especially by the introduction of 'over-stringing', by which the weight of the strings was more evenly distributed.

The nineteenth century was the great age of the pianoforte. The social standing of a family was then indicated by the possession of one. The competition between manufacturers was great and so were the profits for those who were successful in marketing their instruments. The development of new models was a feature of musical life and in an expanding economy new markets were opened up. Pianos were designed for use at sea and in the jungle – and cheap lines were built for school use. That age is past. But the piano remains as a wonderful means of getting to the heart of all kinds of music. Dr Crotch's words are still true.

The piano grew out of the application of a simple single idea : the striking of a string with a hammer.

The development of the idea may be traced technologically – in the mechanical progress of the idea. It may also be traced musically. The styles of Mozart, Beethoven, Clementi, Field, Chopin, Schumann, Liszt, Rachmaninov, Busoni, and many others only developed from an understanding of the qualities of sound which could at any time be produced from the piano. The character of an instrument has much to answer for in respect of music. It is, as was noted in the previous chapter, the task of the composer to show this character.

If you have piano lessons you may now begin to think that there is more in the piano than you thought.

III
The String Quartet

A MONG the great masters of music one stands out because of his unfailing kindness and consideration for other people. This was Joseph Haydn (1733–1809), the Austro-Hungarian composer, who spent the greater part of his life directing the musical arrangements of the household of a great nobleman. His duties consisted of superintending choir and orchestra, conducting performances of church music and of opera, being responsible for chamber and orchestral works of many different kinds, and composing.

After a short period when he was musical director to a Count Ferdinand von Morzin (whose extravagance led to his dismissing

43

his musicians) Haydn was taken into the service of the great Esterházy family. He was first engaged by Prince Paul Esterházy in 1761 and he remained a servant of the family until his death. Apart from the times in later life when he travelled abroad he lived in Eisenstadt or Esterház, where the mansions of the Esterházys were situated, or in Vienna, where they had a town-house.

In those days the aristocracy of Europe cultivated music to a remarkable degree and many musicians found employment in the great houses. Some were unfortunate in the treatment they received from their employers. Others, on the other hand, enjoyed life and found abundant opportunity fully to use their creative talents. Haydn was among the fortunate ones. He was well paid. He was encouraged to compose by the perceptive Prince Nicholas Esterházy – the successor to Prince Paul – who became very proud of, and very attached to, his Music Director. He was able to meet other musicians in Vienna, and often to invite them to meet him in his home. And he had a publishing house – that of the firm of Artaria in Vienna – ready to issue whatever he composed.

A modern composer writes music for the 'public', bearing in mind the audiences of the large concert-hall, or opera-house, or the potentially unlimited and unseen audiences afforded by gramophone, radio, television, or cinema. In the days of Haydn a composer thought most often of a rather special type of audience – generally small in numbers and intimate in character. He was frequently required to compose works which were to be performed in salons or drawing-rooms, where large groups of performers could not be assembled. Or if they could there would be no place for an audience at all. Music of this kind was known as chamber music, and many musicians had the official title of Chamber Music Composer.

When Haydn was a boy in Vienna, where he was a chorister and where he stayed on to shape his career, he would have heard

sonatas for one or two flutes – or oboes, or violins – and harpsichord. For works of this kind, with two high instruments
supported by keyboard (and also a 'cello to make the important
bass line clear), were very popular. Among the composers who
provided famous examples of such sonatas were Corelli, Bach
and Handel.

Violin playing had been brought to a high pitch of perfection
and composers and players exploited the telling and persuasive
tone of the instrument. In ensemble music the lower string
instruments had come off badly. So far as viola players were
concerned they were regarded as merely rather inefficient – and
less good violinists were set to play the viola in the hope that
their errors would escape notice. Cellists, as is shown in pictures
of the period, spent most of their time looking over the shoulder
of the harpsichord player at the music on the stand and support-
ing the harpsichordist's left hand notes. There were, of course,
exceptional cases, but this was the general rule.

In the first example below is shown the opening of a slow
movement of a trio-sonata by the English composer James
Sherard – a doctor by profession but a keen amateur musician –
in the style of Corelli whom he greatly admired. Notice how the
two violins play for a time in parallel movement (at a distance
of a third), and how far away is the 'cello part. The gap was
filled by the chords which the harpsichordist improvised from the
figures under bass line – which is all that he had to play from.

This piece was published about 1711 (Ex. 1). The next
example appeared some fifty years later. It is taken from an
early work of Haydn which now is numbered among his string
quartets. Once again we see how the two violins keep together
(also at a distance of a third) and the 'cello part is still rather
remote. The viola tries to fill the gap, but not very efficiently,
for it merely plays the bass line an octave higher. A harpsichord
is still needed and if this piece was played indoors then Haydn
certainly would have used one (Ex. 2).

The harpsichord part contained only this bass line, the player improvised chords as directed by the figures.

When Haydn was young a musician learned many skills. As a chorister Haydn learned much about singing and the repertoire of church music. When he was on his own and searching both for experience and livelihood he acted as accompanist to the most famous singing-master of the day, Niccolo Porpora. Thus he acquired more knowledge of the technique of singing. Working independently at the craft of composition he had come across the sonatas of Carl Philipp Emanuel Bach (1714–88), which opened a new world of music to him – one in which new forms of expression and construction were apparent. He discovered more about the style and method of this member of the

Bach family by teaching these sonatas to pupils – a very good way of getting to the bottom of anything. Haydn also played the violin and the viola.

Up to the age of twenty-three he was much like many other young musicians in Vienna. He was full of ambition – to be a composer – but needed opportunity. By general consent Haydn is now termed a genius : but unless a genius (which is not a very happy word) is seen to be such he cannot be said to exist. A genius needs a good deal of luck; more, perhaps, than most people.

Haydn's luck in large measure lay in his friendly nature. He was easy to get on with – modest, co-operative, cheerful, and a lively companion; he had interests outside of music, and was popular among sportsmen on account of his enthusiasm for hunting and fishing. His first break came when he was taken on as music master to the family of Baron von Fürnberg. The Baron was not only musical himself, but also of an affable nature. So far as music was concerned he did not stand on ceremony and so long as people could play tolerably he was friendly towards them, whatever their social position.

Baron von Fürnberg had a house in the country; by the Danube, near Melk – a small town, also by the Danube, on the way to another important musical centre – Linz. When he visited his country estate he called in his musical friends. They were the local priest who played the violin, the manager of the estate, also a violinist, and a man named Albrechtsberger who played the 'cello. Provided that someone – a member of the family or the music teacher – was available to play the harpsichord this group could go on happily playing the well-known trio sonatas. If a larger ensemble and fresh musical colouring were wanted, then the horn players who blew their instruments at the hunt or at other open-air occasions were called in.

But Joseph Haydn, in addition to his other accomplishments, also played the viola. He was invited to join in with the other players. He was also encouraged to compose music which could be used from time to time.

Up to a point new musical ideas establish themselves by accident. Baron von Fürnberg liked music, had some musicians to hand, and was ready to give a young composer his chance. Haydn did not set out to revolutionise the world of music, but to take advantage of his opportunity and to give his baron what he wanted. He had already written string trios. He now turned to sets of pieces, of a pleasant and entertaining nature, termed *divertimenti*.

A *divertimento* contained an unspecified number of separate pieces (or movements) and could be written for almost any group of instruments. In his early years Haydn composed many *divertimenti*, some for wind only, some for strings, some for strings and wind, and some for various instruments with keyboard.

More or less by chance he arrived at sets of pieces for two violins, viola, and 'cello. These pieces proved both useful and popular. Since the gap between the two violins at the top and the bass at the bottom was filled in there was no need for the harpsichord to be used. And it was pleasant to hear music that employed the same, consistent, tone of one family of instruments. Such music could be played indoors or out-of-doors. On summer evenings open-air performances were frequent in town or in country.

Haydn had written music for a quartet of string instruments, but, although he referred to his *quadri* (i.e., for four players) he had no idea that he had done anything out of the ordinary. After all there were no binding conventions as to what instruments should or should not be used, and the quartets at first went happily by the side of other *divertimenti*. Their only difference was in their scoring.

Having gained a modest reputation through his connection with one nobleman Haydn capitalised on it and obtained a

permanent post, as director of music to another. He was on the
staff of Count Morzin – whose country-house was at Lukavec in
Bohemia – for two years : from 1759 to 1761. During this period
he went on composing music similar to that which had proved
so successful with the Fürnberg family.

From the period 1755–1760 there have survived thirteen works
by Haydn which are classed as string quartets : six grouped as
Opus 1, from which a brief extract has been given on page 46;
six as Opus 2; and one without an Opus number that was discovered in recent years. Of the quartets one (Op. 1, No. 5)
started its career as a symphony, and two (Op. 2, Nos. 3 and 5)
as *divertimenti* for two horns and strings.

A composer is always anxious to make his music sound effective, or 'right'. To achieve this he must always think carefully
about the handling of his resources, the impact which his music
will make on the ears of his audience, and the character of the
music which the particular audience expects.

The last point is debatable. Is the composer not free to do as
he wishes? No, not really. Even at the present time a composer
has to choose between writing 'modern music' which will put off
a number of his best friends, or 'old-fashioned music' that will
annoy the critics ! Haydn composed either for his friends or for
his patron and employer. He did not write only because he liked
composing, but because it was his livelihood.

Haydn was a very ordinary and (except for music) relatively
uneducated man. His tastes were simple and he spoke with a
broad country accent. His best friends were to be found among
his own class. They loved music because it was part of their life.
But they loved straightforward music. Haydn often had his
closest friends in mind. In what are now counted as the earliest
of his quartets we may appreciate the straightforward quality
of the music. The movements are short, always tuneful, and so
laid out that they will sound effective, if need be, in the open air.
Sometimes we find not only the viola and 'cello playing in

octaves, but also the two violins: this seems to increase the
volume of melodic tone.

From time to time we may appreciate the simplicity of Haydn's
character, his affection for unspoiled people and surroundings,
and his appreciation of the fact that many people's first interest
in music is stirred by what is obvious or commonplace. The
clearest cases, of course, are the familiar slow movement of the
'Surprise' Symphony – with a quiet passage punctuated by percussive explosions – and the equally familiar 'Farewell' Symphony. In these cases the humour is that of a schoolboy; yet we
like Haydn the more because of it.

Humour can be introduced into songs – where words help. It
can be shown in orchestral music because violent contrasts of
tone-colour are easily available. In a string quartet such easy
humour is out of place. Because the tone is relatively small and
uniform, humour – if it appears at all – must be of a more subtle
kind. What we are often aware of is what we call 'good humour'.
This is to be found particularly in the minuet movements and the
finales, when the tunes and the rhythms are immediately appeal-
ing. None more so than this, from the last movement of a quartet
published in 1772 (Ex. 3). The other instruments accompany this
tune with a simple repeated chord.

Ex.3
Rondo-Presto   Haydn, Op.33 No.3
                                                                        etc.

On occasion Haydn remembered the tunes he had heard the
gipsies play. It is said that he often used to visit the gipsy
encampments at night in order to listen to the music of their
fiddlers. In one of his quartets (Op. 20, No. 4) Haydn marks the
minuet 'alla zingarese' – in the gipsy style; but in many cases he
did not do so even though it is clear to the listener that he had

been inspired, either in rhythm or in the treatment of the violin, by gipsy playing.

The directness of much of Haydn's music is a most attractive feature. There is hardly any other great composer who displays such obvious and engaging ideas so frequently as Haydn. Yet it takes more than this to make a great composer. We have some idea of what kind of man Haydn was. We also know what kind of people he liked to be with. But he was, by profession, an Officer of the Household in a prince's palace. Make no mistake, the Esterházys lived in grand style at Eisenstadt and Esterház.

An eighteenth century aristocrat was obliged to pass himself off as a man of taste – even if he had none. As it happens Prince Nicholas was both enthusiastic and well-informed about the arts in general and music in particular. He was a string-player, particularly favouring a now obsolete but very beautiful instrument called the baryton. (Prince Paul had played the violin and the 'cello.) As a man of taste Prince Nicholas had to keep up with other men of taste – in Vienna, in Florence, or Paris. The long and the short of it was that Haydn, whether he wanted to or not, was obliged to compose a great deal of music that was elegant, refined, logical in shape, and stimulating to a keen mind; music that reflected the interest in those qualities which were displayed in other forms in the marvellous new palace that Prince Nicholas built at great expense at Esterház.

As an ambitious composer, and one whose reputation was ever increasing, Haydn was always ready to rise to a challenge. We begin to appreciate his particular genius when we realise that all the qualities of the age in which he lived (as well as others) are reflected in music that was at the same time not only in line with these modern developments but frequently ahead of them. We have the impression, then, of this very ordinary, very attractive man, capable of quite extraordinary achievements in the field of music. The truth is that he thought, and expressed his thoughts, not through words as the majority of people do,

but through music. In this case we may look upon music as a
kind of language.

Anyone who listened to music in Haydn's time believed that
this was the case. So the manner of expressing ideas to the best
advantage through music led to a general acceptance of certain
methods. There were limits to the way in which melodies should
behave; there were limits beyond which harmonies should not
generally stray; there were accepted patterns, or forms. The form
which was confirmed as the most meaningful was that of the
sonata. Haydn as much as anyone was responsible for the matured
sonata-pattern, previously worked at by Carl Philipp Emmanuel
Bach, and for its general acceptance in the mid-eighteenth century.

The form of the sonata – or rather the idea of the sonata, for
no two works in this style are even identical – spread over the
whole field of instrumental music. Haydn composed sonatas for
piano and for other instruments with piano; his symphonies were
sonatas for orchestra; and his chamber music works were of the
same order of design. In such music there was a particular sense
of order and it was this sense of order, prevailing in the music
also of Mozart and Beethoven, that caused men to describe such
music as 'classical'.

Haydn was a busy man. He wrote an enormous amount of
music. It was sensible therefore that so far as instrumental music
was concerned he should think along the same formal lines. The
difference between a symphony and a string quartet is a
difference not of musical quality or structure, but of tone-colour
and the ways in which tone-colours were explored. There is
another difference. Symphonies were written for gala occasions –
when the Prince was entertaining many guests and wished to
show off his whole orchestra : string quartets were for more
private occasions and usually for discerning amateur players.
This being the case the composer, if he so wished, could try
bolder and more unexpected ideas in the latter medium, since
he could often rely on a more understanding audience.

But this is to look ahead. When Haydn first went to the Esterházy family in 1761 the string quartet as such hardly existed. If it did then it was because of those recently composed works of Haydn for that medium. The six which are published as Opus 1 were first printed in 1764 by a Parisian publisher. It was clear to Haydn that – in spite of the uncomplimentary things said about string quartet music by some stick-in-the-mud musicians – there was a future for such works. It is equally clear that he enjoyed writing for this medium – otherwise, since he had much else to do, he would not have continued to do so.

At Eisenstadt Haydn lived in a special wing of the castle known as the 'Musicians' Building'. Since most other of the musicians and their families lived in the same block – rather like a military barracks – there was plenty of opportunity for talking about music and for rehearsing informally. Haydn was very friendly with the first violinist of the establishment, Aloysius Tomasini, and with Joseph Weigl, the cellist. In addition to Tomasini there were four other resident violinists (as well as some 'on call' in the town). Doubtless Haydn took the opportunity to experiment with string quartet music in private – when he might very well have played the viola himself. By 1768 he had written at least eighteen string quartets. In the next year he published a further set of six (such works were usually issued in groups of six), as Opus 3.

Although these quartets are straightforward and not much more complicated than the earlier pioneer works there are some differences to be noted. First of all there is a greater freedom allowed to the instrumentalists, particularly to the first violinist. The first violin part, with an extended range, clearly had someone of the calibre of Tomasini in mind. There are occasional harmonic effects that, when we hear them, cause us to stop and think. There are passages of counterpoint that show how a composer remembers all that he has ever previously heard and how he applies what appears useful in a particular new musical

situation. There are moments when we recall Haydn's love of
nature. One of the most entertaining movements is the minuet of
the third quartet, which because of its 'drone' note is known as
the 'Bagpipe' quartet. But the memorable moments that occur
in these quartets are sometimes of a more reflective kind. There
is one movement in the fifth quartet of this series that has
lingered across the centuries to be known, in many forms and
arrangements, by many people who are probably unaware of
the composer or indeed of the medium of the string quartet.
(Ex. 4.)

Ex.4

There the first violin sings. But it is a quiet song, for the
violin is muted. Below, because the lower strings play *pizzicato*,
it is as though there is some kind of harp accompaniment. This
movement is a kind of serenade. But, although it is related to
music for the voice, it is beautifully thought out in terms of
instrumental music. Nevertheless, this movement, as others of
the set, could be effectively played by a string orchestra, and
often it is.

As he went on experimenting Haydn found out that when
only four solo instruments were used ideas could be presented
that could be shown in no other way. We have already seen how
much the music of today has been influenced by the insistence
of Schoenberg – and other composers – that musical sounds
should never be taken for granted, that each one should be
separately assessed, and that the quality of an instrument should

be borne in mind. Haydn was no less keen in analysing the tonal values of music.

This is shown especially in his treatment of the string quartet. In 1769 he published the quartets of Op. 9; two years later those of Op. 17 were issued. In these works we begin to see how grateful players must have felt to the composer. Each part is interesting in itself, yet the four parts fit together with a consistent texture which sounds like a conversation in music as each player takes up and discusses some idea stated by another. The listener to such works may not easily stand outside the discussion. He finds himself drawn into it, now following the point made by one player, now that made by another. In the earliest of Haydn's quartets the general mood was easy and carefree. More than once in Op. 9 and 17 there is a more serious mood. Two of the quartets are in minor keys. The last movements of two quartets are partly fugal in character.

Here we see Haydn's genius for making use of the whole of his musical experience. Like every composer of the age he was well-trained in the North German techniques of *fugue*, which were strongly maintained in church music but not considered any longer particularly appropriate for 'entertainment' music. Haydn appreciated that in the string quartet there was great scope for musical discussion. He understood that fugue, based on the discussion of a single idea, had something to contribute to the string quartet.

When, in 1772, he composed his next set of quartets, Op. 20, known as the 'Sun' Quartets, he wrote complete fugues as the finales to four out of the six. The fugue which ends the first of this set is a fine and lively example of contrapuntal writing. (Ex. 5.) It begins with violin, and the viola soon enters with a secondary idea (b) which, running against the principal one, plays an important part in the scheme. So too does the innocent-looking scale passage (c). While the main subject (a) is later shown in an inverted form. We learned in the first chapter that

Schoenberg exploited the upside-down form of melodic presentation that we call inversion. But Haydn knew all about this, too. In this fugue Haydn is making use of a form that was then, and often is now, considered as 'serious', or intellectual. Yet he saw no reason why two aspects of music should not be drawn together, and so he built his fugue on a jolly rhythmic pattern.

When the quartets of Op. 20 appeared Wolfgang Mozart was seventeen years of age. He had tried his hand at composing string quartets, under the influence of certain Italian composers. In 1773 he was in Vienna and came across the new set of Haydn. He was greatly impressed and set to work to compose a second set of quartets on his own account. In these quartets (numbered as K. 168–173) there is much evidence of the influence of Haydn : not least of all in the composition of fugal finales for K. 168 and K. 173.

Nine years passed before Haydn published any more string quartets. In 1781 those of Op. 33 were published. By now Haydn was one of the leading figures in European music and as his works came from the publishers they were eagerly subscribed for by music-lovers in many lands. Conscious of the need to sell his works Haydn (who had a keen business sense) sent a circular letter to potential subscribers concerning the set labelled Op. 33, saying that they were composed 'in an entirely new and special manner'. No doubt Haydn, like most other composers at all times, felt when he had completed it that each new work was in some way 'new and special'.

As his string quartets unfold before us we feel how they became more and more capable of expressing Haydn's ideas. Nature was a constant inspiration to Haydn. Often he hints at a scenic background. Nowhere more delicately, more humorously, and more attractively than in the quartet from which the quotation on page 50 is taken. In the first movement of this quartet the first violin has a large number of ornamental notes – that seem to chirp. Appropriately this quartet is popularly known as the 'Bird' quartet. The whole set, because of their dedication to the Grand Duke Paul of Russia, are often called the 'Russian' Quartets.

This set of quartets made a deep impression on Mozart – now also one of the great European masters – and he began to write another series of works of the same order. His last set of string quartets had appeared ten years before. Now, although he showed how much he had learned from Haydn's example, he developed the string quartet medium in his own way. But he was aware of his debt to the older master. He therefore dedicated the quartets (K. 387, 421, 428, 458, 464, 465) to Haydn, and he expressed his thanks to that master in a prefatory letter.

Haydn heard a performance of the last three of these quartets at Mozart's home. Afterwards he spoke to Mozart's father, himself a famous violinist, and said that Wolfgang was the greatest composer he knew. Being a man of deep humility Haydn looked afresh at his own style and in the later years it became clear that just as Mozart was influenced by Haydn so now Haydn was influenced by the younger man.

Because they lived in an age when music could be more readily published and distributed than ever before, when concerts were regularly held in private houses and public buildings, and when the middle-classes as well as the aristocracy were ardent in the practice of chamber music, Haydn and Mozart exercised a

greater and more immediate influence than any previous composers. Their mastery in the field of string quartet made this
branch of musical activity a regular part of the experience of
cultivated music-lovers.

Haydn continued to compose quartets until his last years. The
set of six published in 1787 as Op. 50 were dedicated to the
King of Prussia, who was a 'cellist and for whom Mozart also
wrote some quartets. Further sets were composed for Count
Appony; and for a close friend and pupil Count Erdödy. It is
in the Op. 76 series composed for Erdödy that we find one of
the most celebrated of Haydn's quartet movements. In his
quartets, as in his sonatas and symphonies, he often wrote movements in variation form. In the third quartet of Op. 76 the slow
movement is a set of variations on the hymn tune composed, as
a national anthem, for the Emperor of Austria. Thus the quartet
is commonly referred to as 'the Emperor'.

The last quartet of Haydn was unfinished. Two movements
only remain; but they show us how much richer was the vocabulary of music. In his later quartets Haydn demonstrated that
the forms of classical music were plastic, and that such harmonic
advances had been made that the world of Wagner and the
ultimate break-up of the tonal system was at last in sight. Haydn
made the string quartet the medium through which composers
were to express their deepest feelings and to show their greatest
skills.

Among Beethoven's greatest works are his string quartets.
Brahms was a master of the form. The quartets of Béla Bartók
are regarded as among the masterpieces of the twentieth century.
Schoenberg was drawn to this medium as being the purest in
music.

No one, however, composed so many string quartets as Joseph
Haydn. In no other case is there a collection of such works
covering the whole of a career. Haydn's string quartets show us
the idea of this kind of music. They show us how a simple idea
occurred, and how, under the protection of a great man, it grew
into a great idea.

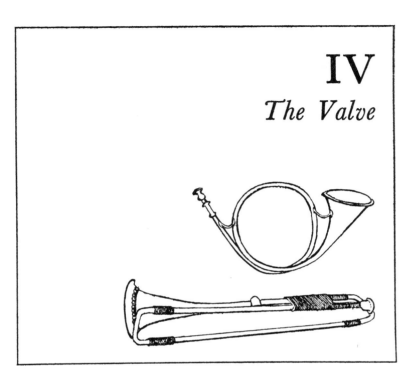

IV

The Valve

I N THE last chapter horns were mentioned. It was also said that in the days of Haydn the same horn that was used in the hunting-field was taken into the more refined setting of the music-room. What kind of instrument was this?

Quite simply a hunting-horn of Haydn's time was a brass tube, with a conical bore, looped round on itself so that it could be more easily carried. Since the length of the tube could be as much as eighteen feet it will be understood why it was necessary to make it with one or more coils. At the thin end of the tube there was a rather flat, funnel-shaped mouthpiece. At the other end the tube flared out into the shape of a bell (See above).

By tightening the lips, pressing them against the mouthpiece, and blowing, the player produced a sound. In fact he could produce a series of sounds. But he could not, except under rather exceptional conditions to be discussed later, produce the scale-wise patterns possible on, say, string or wood-wind instruments. The reason for this lies in the acoustical nature of such an instrument. Let us see what happened when the player blew into his horn.

First of all he set the column of air in the horn vibrating. If he managed to keep his breath flowing steadily into the mouthpiece and not to let his lips wobble he arrived at a consistent musical sound of a particular pitch. The actual pitch depended on the tautness of his lips. The tighter they were the quicker the vibrations set up, and the higher the pitch, which was also dependent on the overall length of the horn.

Let us suppose a tube of sixteen feet in length. If the vibrations run the whole length of the tube the note in Ex. 1 is heard. The vibrations in this case, relatively slow, would be at the rate of sixty-four cycles per second. If, however, only half the speaking length is in operation we would be aware of quicker vibrations and a higher note. In fact (Ex. 2), which is one octave higher than the first note.

A simple tube can only be made to produce certain notes; those notes which come from what is called the harmonic series. This series can be shown as in Ex. 3 on page 61.

Let us suppose that the horn player is able to reproduce all those sounds in the harmonic series. You will notice that the kind of melodic patterns to be heard will have a distinctive character. In the medium register the patterns will be 'gapped'. Anything approaching a scale passage is only possible in the highest register.

Ex.3

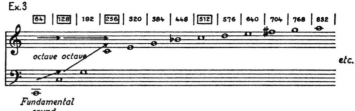

We may bear this in mind and go back to the hunting-field of time past. Only relatively simple calls were needed. Such as were used were taken from those middle-register sounds that were easiest for the players to blow.

Although we have so far referred to the hunting-horn the instrument was used for many different out-of-doors events. Its tone was heard with the military music, during royal and civic pageants, and for religious processions. Most of all in the seventeenth century it was to be encountered in France. To this day the orchestral instrument descended from the early hunting horn is called the 'French Horn'.

During the reign of Louis XIV, who loved and encouraged spectacular pageants, French horn players were very skilful. Visitors to France decided that they too must have horn music. King Charles II, of England, who lived in France during his exile, was much taken with this kind of music, and horn-players were engaged for his team of musicians when he returned to England.

Rather later on a Bohemian nobleman, Count Franz von Spork, heard the horn in France and he liked the sound of it. More or less at once he made two of his servants learn to play. When he went back to Bohemia he showed off the new, and strange, skills of his servants, and also the instruments he had bought.

By the end of the seventeenth century instrument-makers in various parts of Europe were busy making horns. Very soon the horn found its way into the orchestra.

If a composer had written an opera and there was a hunting scene then the tone of the horn was the very thing to encourage an audience to believe in what was happening on the stage. The imaginative listener shut his eyes, perhaps, as he heard the patterns of horn sounds that were almost identical with those to be heard out-of-doors. He no longer thought about the theatre in which he was sitting, but about the fields and woods among which he now thought himself to be chasing the fox, or the deer, or the wild boar. Many instruments found their way into the orchestra because they possessed some particular quality that reflected what goes on in the world in general.

You have only to hear a few notes blown on a trumpet to feel excited. It is no wonder that trumpets were for hundreds of years invaluable on state and military occasions. We hear trumpet-calls – often quite elaborate ones – when events like a coronation, the opening of a great assembly, or the consecration of a church or cathedral, take place. These trumpet calls are termed fanfares. And when you hear a fanfare you will notice that the melodic patterns are frequently gapped, like those of the horn. That is because the old form of trumpet, like the horn, could only be made to produce the sounds of the harmonic series.

There is a considerable difference between the kind of tone coming from the horn on the one hand and the trumpet on the other. This is due to differences in shape of mouthpiece, in bore of tube, and in length. The trumpet mouthpiece is cup-shaped. Its tube is cylindrical until it reaches the end, where it flares out again into the shape of a bell. Because the trumpet is shorter than the horn, the pitch is higher. All these factors also make for a distinctive brilliance of tone.

Horns and trumpets belong to the family of brass instruments. The trumpets play high notes. The horns, generally speaking, play middle register notes. Down below, to play the bass notes, is the trombone. This too is an old instrument and it was, perhaps, valued more in the early days of instrumental ensemble than it is now. Within the limits of its range the trombone, because of its construction, could play any note.

If you look at a trombonist as he is playing you will notice that he seems to have to possess more agility than most other players in the orchestra (except perhaps the percussion players). While he holds his instrument with one hand the other is kept busy pushing a length of tubing to and fro. (Diagram 1.) The

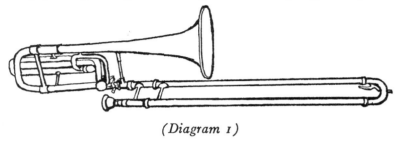

(Diagram 1)

trombone consists of two parallel tubes, over which a third, U-shaped, and moveable tube is fixed. There is, then, a tube of which the length can be varied.

The trombone-player can in fact move his 'slide' into seven different positions, so that each position may give a different note of the chromatic scale. Seven notes are not many. But if we remember what we have learned about the harmonic series it will be realised that each of the seven *fundamental* notes (as they are called) will give its own series of harmonics. This explains why the trombone can cover all the notes of a scale.

Because of this the trombone – or sackbut as it was formerly called – was specially favoured. It was given proper tunes to play! In the seventeenth and eighteenth centuries the trombone was not thought of specially as a loud instrument. Often used in the accompaniment of voices it was kept at a medium level of loudness. Some of the finest music of the seventeenth century to show the then versatility of the trombone was composed for ensembles of these instruments by the Venetian musician Giovanni Gabrieli (1557–1612). Not long after this time, however, the trombone group was pushed into the background by the development of the violin family and by the fact that orchestras were based on the uniformity of tone which the complete string ensemble provided.

Before the seventeenth century there was no orchestra as we now know it. There were families of instruments made in different sizes and the composer either wrote for one of these families – of viola, or recorders, or trombones, for instance – or he left anyone who was directing a performance to take instruments out of the different families and put them together in any way he pleased. With the supremacy of the violin group, however, the earliest music that you are likely to hear in a concert comes from the late seventeenth or the early eighteenth centuries. You will notice that strings predominate. Oboes and bassoons and flutes may be used from time to time. But not, as a rule, brass instruments. These were kept where they had always tended to belong, to the open air.

When the majority of orchestral players were employed at the courts of the nobility the aristocrats of the profession were the string players. Next to them in esteem were the oboists and bassoonists. The trumpet, horn, and trombone players were classified as the 'field-music'. When they were required, for an opera, or perhaps an oratorio, they were brought away from their usual open-air duties, but sent back as soon as they had played what was required of them in theatre orchestra. The idea that brass players were somehow of a lower social order persisted almost to modern times.

You will appreciate the reason. Violinists (who were often pampered) could play almost anything, however difficult it might be. They were able to show off in sonatas and concertos. There are many, many violin sonatas and concertos of the later

seventeenth and early eighteenth centuries. But not very many
for brass instruments.

Composers, however, disliked there being fine, exhilarating,
even uplifting sounds which they could not use. Bit by bit the
trumpet pushed its way into the orchestra. Not as a regular
member, but as an honoured guest on special occasions.
Trumpeters, frustrated by not being able to play tunes like
everyone else, developed a special technique. They specialised in
the higher register, where the harmonies were close together.
Purcell, Handel, and Bach wrote splendid high trumpet parts.
A familiar and notable example is in 'The Trumpet shall sound'
in Handel's oratorio *Messiah*. The text shows why the trumpet
had to be used. There is also to be remembered the striking effect
of trumpets in the 'Hallelujah' chorus in the same oratorio.

As with trumpets so with horns. And here we remember the
marvellous horn parts – as in the first of the Brandenburg
Concertos – that Bach composed; very high, and now, to all but
the most expert of modern players, very difficult. The trombones
were slower to receive recognition in the orchestra of this period :
but Handel again used them to great effect in his 'Dead March'
– and in other movements – in the oratorio *Saul*.

When we have gained experience we are quickly able to tell
if a piece of music we hear is of the period of Handel or Bach.
We are also able to tell whether a piece of music belongs to the
period in which Haydn and Mozart were the greatest news. We
know, from Chapter 3, what kind of qualities were extracted in
the latter period. A little reasoning will show that the brass
instruments once again were temporarily demoted.

A trumpet part by Handel looks like this (Ex. 4).

Ex.4 Andante allegro   *from Saul*

etc.

A trumpet part by Haydn looks like this (Ex. 5).

A horn part by Bach looks like this (Ex. 6).

and a horn part in a symphony by Mozart looks like this (Ex. 7).

With Haydn and Mozart we find ourselves once again back with the patterns of notes that belong to the natural harmonic series.

If you look at the full score from which the conductor directs a performance of a work (unless he relies on his memory), or at a miniature score, you will find that the trumpets and the horns have information like this:

Trumpets in B♭; in C; in F.
Horns in F; in E♭; in D; in C.

What does that mean?

Simply this: that the trumpet or the horn was supplied with extra lengths of coiled tube which could be fixed to the instrument so that it could play harmonic series based on a different fundamental note than the one given by the original length of tubing. These additions were called crooks (from their shape).

With this aid the player could more or less fit into any key in which the orchestra happened to be playing. It should be remembered that in spite of Bach's efforts to show how all the major and minor keys could be used (see Chapter 6) there was for a long time a tendency only to use keys with a few sharps or flats.

But still, compare the Haydn and Mozart trumpet and horn parts with any of the woodwind and string parts and you will see that the trumpets and horn players must have felt still rather underprivileged!

This business of slides and crooks seems at first unnecessarily complicated, for while a brass instrument is a tube, so is a woodwind instrument. And woodwind instruments managed to keep abreast of musical development. In the eighteenth century they had their quota of sonatas and concertos. In the case of woodwind instruments the speaking length of the tube was varied by the holes bored in the side, which the player covered with his fingers, or, later on, with pads operated by finger-keys. Did no one think of applying this principle to, say, the trumpet?

The answer is yes. Because of this we have one of the most attractive of all concertos: that in E flat, for trumpet, by Haydn. The Court Trumpeter in Vienna – during the last part of Haydn's life was Anton Weidinger. Being of an inventive frame of mind he decided to see what would happen if he did try to bore holes in the instrument and open or close them by the use of keys. Having made such an instrument he thought that the best way of testing it was by inviting composers to write some music specially for him. Haydn, always ready to oblige a friend, wrote his concerto in the year 1796. Other composers followed suit, among them Johann Hummel, who succeeded Haydn as Director of Music to the Esterházy family.

The keyed trumpet proved a boon to military bands in Austria and also in Italy where it was used until well into the nineteenth century. Unfortunately the tone is not so rich as that of the

natural trumpet and it never made its way into the orchestra.
Thus we find that the trumpet and horn parts of Beethoven *look*
like those of Haydn and Mozart. That they often sound rather
different is due not to the notes but to the way in which Beethoven wrote them. Hardly ever did he fail to use them
dramatically. The most dramatic use of trumpets by Beethoven
was in one of the overtures to his opera *Fidelio* (in which the
heroine was Leonora) known as 'Leonora No. 3', where a trumpet
sounds a fanfare at a distance from the main body of the
orchestra.

Beethoven, keenly aware of the dramatic possibilities of brass
music, brought the trombone into the symphony orchestra in his
Fifth Symphony.

It now becomes important to find out what people expected
of music in the first part of the nineteenth century. We have seen
how the character of music changed during Haydn's lifetime –
partly but not entirely through the genius of Haydn himself. The
change was all in one direction, towards a greater degree of
expressiveness. The more expressive music became the more it
seemed to describe life in its many phases. The greater the
number of people interested in music the greater the importance
of this matter of explanation.

Haydn and Mozart were in the first place expected to address
a select body of music-lovers. Towards the end of their careers,
however, they were aware of what we would now call a mass
audience. Beethoven much more consciously believed in his
mission to write music for the many rather than the few. This
being the case he had to make sure that he could hold the attention of his audiences. He tried to do this by making his larger
works directly relevant to the feelings and emotions and ideals
he knew to exist, and which in due course he expected to be
within the experience of everybody. He knew the great impact
that the instruments of the orchestra could make. Therefore he
exploited instrumental colours.

Other composers, now less well known, did the same. Among
the composers to whom Beethoven was indebted were François
Gossec (1734–1829), and Etienne-Nicolas Méhul (1763–1817),
prominent musicians in France during the era of the French
Revolution. Both were ardent in their pursuit of revolutionary
principles and both composed works which were designed to
forward revolutionary ideals. They therefore tried to popularise
music, to make it accessible to all people, so that they could the
more readily convey their thoughts. Apart from choosing revolutionary subjects these composers realised that if they wished to
make a direct appeal they must make extensive use of the stirring
qualities of wind instruments.

Gossec composed a fine Funeral March in honour of Honoré
Mirabeau, in which the ideas of nobility and sadness were laid
out in dramatically contrasted musical colours and rhythms. A
feature of this music is the colour of the gong. Another composer
who composed a Funeral March (in memory of one of the
revolutionary generals) was Luigi Cherubini (1760–1842). Such
works were the inspiration of the Funeral Marches (including
those of Beethoven and Chopin) of the nineteenth century.

Gossec's popularisation of the symphony led him at an early
stage in the history of the symphony to compose an extensive
'Hunting Symphony' (1776), in which wind instruments played
a prominent part. This was 'programme music' and Gossec was
a pioneer in this field. Méhul also helped to develop an appreciation of the evocative qualities of instruments that had, in a sense,
been neglected. In the overture to his opera, *The Young Henry*
(1797), he used four horns. An interesting work of two years
earlier was a fine overture for wind instruments only. The
methods of Gossec, Méhul, and Cherubini, as well as their ideals,
were important insofar as Beethoven's development as a composer was concerned. But their revelation of new musical colours
was of wider significance. It became imperative to ensure that
brass instruments could play their full part in the expansion of

musical appreciation. This is where technological ability was indispensible.

The composer knows what he wants from an instrument. The perceptive inventor understands what the composer is driving at. This is what happened in the case of the pianoforte. And now in the case of brass instruments other than the trombone.

Crooks enabled a player to alter the length of his tube. But changing crooks took time. What was needed was some kind of built-in device for making such alteration possible. As is so often the case we do not know exactly who was the first to apply such a device. The choice lies between Heinrich Stölzel and Friedrich Blühmel. Since they came together and collaborated it does not much matter.

Stölzel was a horn-player in a German court orchestra. Blühmel played in a miners' wind-band. After independent experiments the two men patented a piston valve in 1818 which was taken up and used by an instrument maker named Schuster in Carlsruhe. The valve mechanism meant that what had previously been done very cumbersomely by means of crooks was now achieved by lengths of tubing now incorporated within the instrument and controlled by the pistons operated by the player's fingers.

The most convenient arrangement allowed for three valves. The first gave sufficient extra tubing to lower the pitch by a half – or semi-tone; the second allowed two half-tones – or one full tone; the third three half-tones. The valves could be used separately or in combination. (Diagram 2.)

As in the case of the piano when a new mechanical device came on to the market there was a general move to adopt it and then to modify it. The wind instrument market was profitable. There were military bands, but there were also bands of wind-players attached to social, industrial, and political associations. And there was the orchestra.

We are, perhaps, inclined to think of the development of

music in too restricted terms. The importance of the numerous amateur wind-bands of Britain, Germany, and America, in helping to spread a love of music cannot be over-estimated. These players – before long attempting arrangements of popular 'classical' items – did as much as anyone to carry out the intention of Beethoven that music should be as widely appreciated as possible.

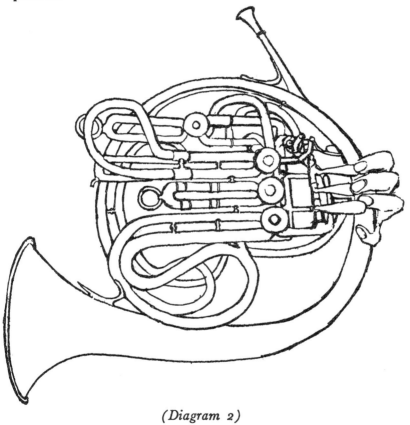

(Diagram 2)

When the valve principle was applied it needed a great deal of modification in order to secure perfect intonation. Among those who experimented with different designs were Leopold Uhlmann, an instrument-maker of Vienna, and Pierre-Jean Meifred, the first to play a piece on the valve-horn at a public concert in Paris. Like the virtuoso players of earlier times anxious to show off a new instrument Meifred composed his own music. The most important name in the nineteenth century development of brass instruments, however, was that of Adolphe Sax (1814–94).

The Sax family originated in Belgium. Charles Joseph Sax (1791–1865) established himself as an instrument-manufacturer in Brussels. Of his eleven children Adolphe showed much musical talent and graduated as flautist and clarinettist from the School of Music in Brussels. Adolphe saw more opportunity in Paris than in Brussels and settled there in 1842. He had an ear for the colours of wind instruments and became friendly with two composers who also were conscious of what could be done with them. One was Hector Berlioz (1803–69), the other Jacques Halévy (1799–1862). In 1844 Sax showed instruments he had made at the Paris Exhibition of that year and won high honours.

Meanwhile he was applying the valve principle to an instrument only used in military music. The result of his experiments was the group of instruments known as 'saxhorns'. This group, covering the whole range of notes available to brass instruments, is now the foundation of the British brass band. Saxhorns, round in tone and easier to play than French horns, came out at a convenient time. The French army was about to re-equip its music-corps, and the saxhorns were a godsend. Sax, to the annoyance of most other manufacturers, obtained a virtual monopoly to supply the army.

A year after he had put the saxhorn on the market Sax produced an even more familiar instrument – the saxophone. This was a single-reed metal instrument with a conical bore. Sax, it is suggested, was looking for some tone that would blend with

the reed instruments on the one hand and with the brass
instruments on the other.

So far as the valved instruments were concerned their full
potentialities were most extensively displayed by Richard
Wagner, who demanded a large expansion of the orchestral
brass section. In his cycle of music-dramas entitled *The Ring* he
asked for eight horns, four tubas, three trumpets, double bass
tuba and brass trumpet – as well as four trombones and bass
trombone. The number of instruments – although showing a
general tendency of the period towards extravagance – is not so
important as what was done with them. Here is a passage from
Siegfried in which the chromatic notes would have been impossible before the invention of the valve : (**Ex. 8**).

Ex. 8   (Brass)

This passage is known as the "Heavenly Wanderer,"
a Leitmotiv (see Chapter 12)

The upgrading of brass instruments, within the orchestra, gave
rise to a new respect for brass players among whom new
standards of virtuosity were established. It also had its effect on
the orchestra as a whole. It was not enough to include a full
brass section in the orchestra. In order to maintain balance it
became necessary to increase the numbers of players in other
sections – notably, of course, the strings. Such increases meant
that other effects, often to be obtained by dividing the strings
into more parts than the previously used four, were to be
obtained.

Orchestral music at the beginning of the nineteenth century

was one thing. At the end it was another. At the end of the century we meet Tchaikovsky, Dvorák, Richard Strauss, Anton Bruckner, Gustav Mahler, and Edward Elgar. These masters of the orchestra still furnish a large part of the general concert repertoire. Each discovered how to use to the full the resources of the modern orchestra, not least of all the brass section. Not one would have composed the music he did if the valve had not been invented and perfected during his lifetime.

In the course of time many inventions affected the nature of music. In most cases we do not know who was responsible for them in the first place. We do not know who first discovered how to make music with a reed – though legend ascribes the discovery to 'the great god Pan'. We do not know who first applied a bow to a stringed instrument – though a sculpture of the twelfth century in the minster in Zürich shows a player using a bow. Yet those who did make these discoveries and applied their inventive powers to their application should be among the great names in music. Therefore, Adolphe Sax, who applied the valve principle so widely, deserves to be reckoned among the great musicians – or, perhaps better, among the great makers of music, who helped others to make music.

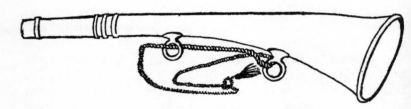

V

St. Gregory
and a system of scales

THE basis of an ordered society is organisation. The question is: who is going to do the organising? To this another question must be added: to what end? There is, of course, trouble when those who are to be organised object either to the organisers or to the purpose or the method of organisation. What the organiser hopes is that he will have sufficient power to over-ride any objections.

Where do musicians and music come into this? At first it might appear that the composer is one of the few lucky people in the world who is able to do as he pleases. Alas! this is a long way from the truth, as we have already begun to appreciate in the previous chapters. His freedom is limited in many ways. Because he must live he must reckon with economic factors. Some one, or some institution, must pay him for his work. It is seldom that a composer can afford not to pay attention to the likes and dislikes of those who he hopes will support him. If he tries too hard to give people what they think they want he probably ends up by writing not very good music. If he does not try hard enough and goes too far away from the taste of the time very few will listen to what he composes.

Those who are not musicians by vocation often think they know more about it than those who are. Maybe they do. If they are unimportant it does not very much matter. If, on the other hand, they exercise influence it matters a lot. It should be said here that the musician, who supplies what is clearly a necessary amenity of life, does his own career disservice if he is unwilling to consider other points of view than his own. But in the end in deciding what he will do he must, like every other citizen, consult his conscience.

The Greek philosopher, Plato, considered that musicians should be kept under control and that music, especially in education, should be carefully regulated. It was his view that music had a strong effect on character. This idea has persisted, in different forms, down to the present day. It will no doubt continue to persist.

The present Chinese government discourages Western music and encourages what it rather incorrectly calls folk music. By folk music in this context is meant simple songs in praise of certain political principles, or in honour of and descriptive of work. The idea is, that in the first case political loyalty will be strengthened, and that in the second people will work with more vigour. Because it was thought to have a weakening effect on character and morale the music of Schoenberg was once banned in Germany by government order. Operas have always tended to tread on shaky ground. They are especially vulnerable because of their use of words. The text of Mozart's *Marriage of Figaro* was severely scrutinised before it passed the Austrian censorship.

The most serious arguments about the use of music have, however, always taken place among religious leaders.

If you go into a Calvinist church you hear one kind of music. If you go into a Lutheran church you hear another kind of music. If you go into a Roman Catholic church there is a third kind of music to be sampled. In the Church of England, and allied Episcopalian churches throughout the world, it is possible to hear some or all of the previous types mixed together – as well as another more or less distinctive idiom.

As you listen to music which has a religious purpose you will find yourself moved in different ways. The plain psalm-tunes of the Calvinists may repel you by their apparent monotony; on the other hand they may inspire you (as they were supposed to do) by the strength of their simplicity. You will not, I think, feel that you are being entertained. You may not 'like' a Catholic hymn chanted without harmony and in a melodic style that will almost certainly sound unfamiliar : but you may be moved by what seems to be an element of mystery in the music. There is music at revivalist meetings, such as those of Dr Billy Graham. This may very well sound attractive, because it is not very far moved from the idioms of certain popular forms of music.

If you happen to belong to a particular faith, and if you have strong feelings about it, you will probably think that the music belonging to that faith has some kind of superiority. You may not consciously think this; but deep down you will have some sort of feeling to that effect.

The further back into history we go the more important different styles of religious music become, because, of course, religion itself was a much more important factor. The further back we go the more illiteracy we meet. Among illiterate, or relatively illiterate people, pictures and music, images and colourful and dramatic ceremony, play a most important part in forming ideas.

All these artistic means were extensively used by the Catholic church. It is significant that when the Reformation came it was when many more people were literate than in former times. This being so ideas were the basis of discussion, or argument, and the necessity for presenting them indirectly – through the arts – seemed rather less.

For many centuries, however, the Catholic church, with its headquarters in Rome, was the only Christian body in Western Europe. Because it made great use of music it affected the whole development of music. That it did so was in the first place a matter of organisation.

The music of the Roman church came from many sources. The early Christians were to be found among the Jewish people and they maintained Jewish ritual musical practices. They sang hymns and they sang psalms. With the spread of Christianity, churches were founded in the Middle Eastern countries, in North Africa, as well as in Southern and Eastern Europe.

Each of these churches maintained its own traditions, which were rooted in pre-Christian practices and customs. If you had gone to Constantinople you would have heard music for hymns and psalms that had inherited some of the characteristics of ancient Greek music, as well as other derived from that of the Jewish temple. If on the other hand you had penetrated into Ethiopia you would have heard quite different music. You would have heard priests singing in a strange, even wild, idiom for hours on end, and with such fervour that they drove themselves into a state of exhaustion. You would have seen other priests dancing liturgical dances, to the accompaniment of rattles and drums. The idea of the 'sacred dance', in a Christian setting, has been brought back, in various ways, into contemporary music, often to its enrichment. Whether in rhythmic pattern, or heavily percussive instrumentation we may readily appreciate this in such works as Gustav Holst's *Hymn of Jesus*, Igor Stravinsky's *Symphony of Psalms*, Benjamin Britten's *St Nicholas*, Leo Bernstein's *Chichester Psalms*, while even in the greatest of the familiar and traditional oratorios of Bach and Handel there are barely disguised dance movements. The religious aspect of the dance, deeply rooted in psychological needs, carries over, as we shall see, into the ballet.

There was one form of church music in France, another in Spain, another in Milan, and yet another in Rome. These forms were highly cultivated and many fine melodies were composed. Behind these European melodies lay the influence of Greek music; because many Greeks had settled in communities in Italy during the first two centuries or so of the Christian era.

In the course of time the city of Rome became the undisputed centre of Christianity, and Roman methods and ideas were imposed throughout the Christian world. By the seventh century a certain uniformity began to prevail in the field of church music.

Missionary priests went far afield to bring distant lands into conformity with Rome. St Augustine, for example, went to England. Missionary priests took with them sacred books so that those they converted could follow the approved practices. They also took with them the most important of the songs of the church, for it was well established that these enabled people to remember the words of the faith.

Not long after the missionary fathers others, with more special tasks, followed. Among these not the least important were the singing-teachers, who set up schools of music.

All this activity was at first directed by one man – one of the greatest organisers of his time. This was the Pope Gregory I, known as Gregory the Great, who reigned at the end of the sixth and the beginning of the seventh centuries. Such was his importance in respect of music that the most significant and characteristic music of the Catholic church is to this day known as the 'Gregorian Chant'.

The discipline of religion required all the members of religious bodies to do the same thing at the same time. The services of the Catholic Church were drawn up to this end, and the monastic institutions were set up in the first place to ensure that the routine of prayer – and praise – was decently kept up. This routine was a matter of words, and of formalised actions.

Words, however, were not quite independent. They were taken away from normal speech and made to sound more impressive by being intoned.

The intonation of a psalm, or a response, or of a portion of the Mass, from one angle appeared as a special kind of speech, or declamation, with regular rise and fall of the voice. The rise and fall (what otherwise we would call the shape of the melody) had both purpose and meaning : for the words were brought to life, some were emphasised more than others, and even if the individual words could not be distinguished the worshipper knew what they were because he recognised the distinctive rising and falling patterns. In certain African languages, which are described as 'tonal', exact differences of pitch within individual words are essential to the particular word idea, and precisely define meaning. This is not the case with European languages, but when words and music are joined together as intimately as was the case with the early Christian chant it is nearly so.

If we look at the chanted psalm or response from another angle we recognise it as music. We even begin to use the words 'like' and 'dislike' to show our reactions. If we do we are using wrong terms. In the first instance the music of a sect (however large the sect) is the private property of that sect and there for the enforcement of uniformity, not for the purpose of entertainment.

Now Pope Gregory the Great was concerned with this matter of uniformity. He was also concerned that the Church should be a universal church. It is not likely that he was interested in providing entertainment. In fact he was, we may presume, like any other Father of the Church, intent on preventing music becoming an end in itself. Therefore neither singing in parts nor instrumental accompanists were encouraged.

When Gregory became Pope there were many different kinds of church song. In the centuries that followed his reign there there was but one system according to which church song might be composed. The idea of a musical style was therefore established: the first of the different styles that have come to characterise the Western musical tradition.

Now it is important to realise that actual music exists before a style can be said to do so. Thus a scheme, or a theory, is evolved because there is music to make it possible. The 'rules' of musical composition deal with what has taken place, not with what is going to take place. The organiser is not really an innovator, but one who brings some order into a not always orderly situation. Gregory the Great, insofar as he was an organiser in the field of music, dealt with a great mass of compositions that were in common use.

Let us look at this music more closely. It divided into two main tyes. The one was termed 'responsorial', the other 'antiphonal'. The first type was the older, and grew up in this way. In the early days of Christian worship the words (as of a psalm) were delivered in a monotone, or near monotone, by a solo voice (usually of a priest). This method not only came from the practices of earlier ritual, but also, though indirectly, had a relationship with the *recitative* of later time. When the soloist had intoned a phrase it became customary for the rest of the congregation to sing a simple refrain, or response. The practice remains in many churches to the present day.

In the course of time, up to and well beyond the time of Gregory the Great, music of this kind grew very elaborate. For there were schools of song which made it their aim to perfect the music – and its performance – of the Church.

By the side of the response type of performance there

developed the antiphonal style. Here instead of there being soloist and choir were two alternating choirs. One of the choirs sang the first phrase : the other sang the answering phrase. This method was suggested by the structure of the words of the psalms (the basis of church music), where each verse consists of two phrases that balance each other. The two main phrases were best given by two different kinds of voice, by those of men on the one hand and those of boys or of women on the other.

The refrain used in the response method became important in its own right and eventually was placed before as well as after the verse of the psalm. The next stop was the freeing of the refrain from its first function and its establishment as an independent combination of words and, increasingly, ornate music.

Already we begin to see the shape of musical patterns that in one way or another exercised a great influence on the later development of musical ideas. Most important was the idea of tonality.

In the simpler recitative type of singing the monotoned note at, or near, the beginning was important – because it was the most conspicuous. In the more complex song-form that emerged it was the last sound – the *final* – that assumed the greatest importance. This was a coming-home sound. It marked the end of a lengthy musical statement as does a full stop in writing.

When Pope Gregory (or those who worked towards the schemes and organisations with which he is credited) looked at the mass of music in general they discovered that certain groupings of notes in the melodies of the church songs were more common than others. This being the case they classified them. Just as the major and minor scales as we call them show the sound patterns that occur in the music of one period so do the modes (as they were called) into which the early scholars put their findings show the main melodic principles of another.

There were four pairs of modes, each pair sharing the same final note :

I (Ex. 2a) Dorian II (Ex. 2a′) Hypo-Dorian
III (Ex. b) Phrygian IV (Ex. b′) Hypo-Phygian
V (Ex. c) Lydian VI (Ex. c′) Hypo-Lydian
VII (Ex. d) Mixolydian VIII (Ex. d′) Hypo-Mixolydian
At a later stage these were added :
IX (Ex. e) Aeolian X (Ex. e′) Hypo-Aeolian
XI (Ex. f) Ionian XII (Ex. f′) Hypo-Ionian

Ex. 2

In each of the modes on the right hand side the semi-tones
and tones fall in different places, whereas in the more modern
scales the small intervals – the half – or semi-tones, and the larger
intervals, or tones, always occur in the same places. If you sing
(or play) these modes you will find that each has its own distinctive character on account of the lay-out of tone and semi-tone.
You will also notice that only two show the distinctive semi-tonal

(*te-doh'*) ending of the major (or the minor) scale. The first of these – the 'Lydian' – sounds like a major scale with a 'wrongnote'; the second, the 'Ionian', is in fact exactly the same as a major scale – but this mode was not one of the 'classical' modes of St Gregory's time.

At this point if you so wish you may make up some melodies, using the notes of the modes. You will be surprised that they sound in a sense almost 'modern'. To be exact they will seem more modern because less familiar. So we learn again that what is taken as up-to-date is, quite often, based on some old and largely forgotten principle.

It is one thing to draw up a scheme. It is another to make it effective. We have arrived at the Gregorian Modes and at a large body of church music that was called Gregorian. How did this style of music become the dominant style of the Western world?

Pope Gregory we may now leave behind. If the idea of reforming and tidying up church music was not his alone he was traditionally given the credit for it.

When St Augustine came to England in the year 596 he brought with him a number of priests competent in the art of church music. Only twenty-five years after the death of Pope Gregory there was a song-school attached to the monastery at Canterbury where Gregorian music was practised. Not long afterwards a great singing-master from Rome, whose name was John, came to England. After working in different parts of the country he made his headquarters at Wearmouth in the county of Durham, and many came to learn from him.

The same thing happened all over Western Europe. Experts in the art of Roman church music established themselves and set up schools of song, which acted as centres of learning. There was one such school at the monastery of Corvey, near Amiens, in France. In due course monks from Corvey went into Germany where they founded the great abbey at Corvei, on the River

Weser, and this too became a centre of music. Some parts of the eighth-century church at Corvei are still to be seen.

Pepin and Charlemagne, great organisers, reigned during the eighth century, and they were ardent in their efforts on behalf of church music. They were inspired by a love of music. But they were anxious to unify Europe, and saw that music could help bring this about. Of all the famous teaching establishments of those times none was more important than that at the Abbey of St Gallen, in Switzerland. In the library of the present Abbey are to be seen some of the most precious of early musical documents : service books which contain the musical notation of those times.

Music was one part of a movement that became increasingly powerful in the centuries that lay between those two great architects of European thought and organisation, Gregory and Charlemagne. The latter was inspired by the same ideas as the former. The dominant idea was of order. By the ninth century an age of cultural darkness was ended. We may, indeed, see parallels with the later Renaissance. Not least of all in the development of a new and magnificent style of architecture, which in many details reflected the characteristics of the architectural style of classical Rome.

Churches were built in the style of older basilicas. The cloister, round which the household buildings were grouped, became a feature of monastic properties. Among the most famous 'Gregorian' churches in England were those founded by St Wilfrid at Hexham, York, and Ripon. At a later date came the great churches (of which only ruins remain) of St Augustine's Abbey in Canterbury, and of Glastonbury. Such places were built to the glory of God, but for the performance of ritual and of music. The Gregorian concept was not of music alone, but of music in relation to its use and setting. That is why this idea in particular was a 'great idea'.

The principles of so-called Gregorian music became more

comprehensive than could ever have been foreseen. For the whole
of music became affected by these principles. Just how far-
reaching were their effects may be seen from the fact that one
of the great works for organ composed by Johann Sebastian Bach
was called the *'Dorian' Toccata and Fugue*. This was because
the two parts of the work reflected something of the character
of the old Gregorian mode. Although the music is as we would
now say generally in the key of D minor the signature of this
key is not shown by Bach. This composer was acclimatised to
the feel of the modes because so many of the chorales of the
Lutheran Church with which he had been familiar since boyhood were derived from modal melodies that had belonged to
the pre-Reformation Church.

One of these melodies, later set to the words of the Lord's
Prayer, is set at the head of this chapter. But this is the way in
which Bach treated these notes in a variation – or a *Chorale
Prelude* – on the theme. (Ex. 3.)

In this way the Gregorian influence, unmistakably, came down
across more than a thousand years. But it was not the only way.

We often speak of 'sacred' and 'secular' music. There have
always been those who have tried to keep the two kinds of music
apart from each other. But however hard this has been tried the
effort has sooner or later met with failure. Musicians use their ears!

In the great melodies of the church of the Middle Ages there

were ideas that had once come out of secular music, especially
out of folk music. In due course patterns of musical speech that
had become accepted in Church music passed into the common
musical language. So we find that many of the folk melodies of
Europe that are still familiar were constructed according to the
principles of the modes. Many tunes are to be discovered which
are in the Dorian and Aeolian Modes, which seem to have been
especially popular. Modal melodies therefore turn up in unexpected places.

Ex.4   English Nursery Song

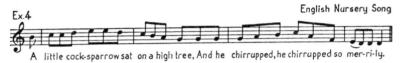

A little cock-sparrow sat on a high tree, And he chirrupped, he chirrupped so mer-ri-ly.

Pope Gregory would have been surprised to have found this
'Dorian' ending (Ex. 5) in a nursery song collected and published
in his *Baby's Bouquet* (1879) by Walter Crane. Maybe he would
have been even more surprised to have found a group of lively
sailors wondering, 'What shall we do with the drunken sailor?' –
also in the Dorian Mode. He would have been less surprised to
have found the English, victorious after the Battle of Agincourt
(1415), singing the now famous 'Agincourt Song' in the same
mode. For the composers of that day, when required to make
up such pieces, naturally employed the techniques that had been
refined through long usage in church.

We have seen in the first chapter how, not so very long ago,
composers felt that music was at a point of crisis. Many asked,
'Where do we go from here?' Some looked sideways, like
Debussy and Seriabin and, at first, Schoenberg, to see if new
formulas could be found by extending familiar and accepted
principles of tonality. Some, like the second period Schoenberg,
or the most interesting and original American composer Charles
Ives, looked ahead to find the music of the present as it were in
the future. Others looked back.

Of the composers who sought to produce a new, and more realistic, music of the present from out of the mists of the past, a number determined to renew melodic vigour from modal sources.

During the Romantic movement of the nineteenth century a new attitude to melodies of modal type began to prevail. Such melodies, because of their associations with the age-old tradition of the Catholic Church, tended to suggest something 'old'. In one of his last works – a choral work for a Catholic church festival in Liège, entitled *Lauda Sion* – Mendelssohn introduced a modal flavour. The English composer Samuel Wesley composed a number of works in which he not only sought to bring back the sterner contrapuntal manner of choral writing that had prevailed in the 'golden age' of church choral music – the sixteenth century – but also the austere quality thought to belong to the Gregorian melodic system. In one of his works, *In Exitu Israel* (The passage of the Israelites out of Pharaoh's Egypt), he made the traditional plainsong theme the basis of his music.

English composers of later time took to the modal idiom in a big way. It seemed first to provide a way of escape from the 'German' idioms that had long held sway. But second, since the English have a tendency to be romantically minded about their own past, it seemed nicely national in a not too provocative way. The choral works, of Vaughan Williams, especially those for church use, are heavily modal. The same influence is to be found in the music of Gustav Holst. Even at the present time the importance of plainsong, because of its evocative and mystical quality, is prominent in two of Britten's recent works – *Curlew River* and *The Burning Fiery Furnace*.

That modal characteristics marked folk music meant that composers with a strong sense of national pride also composed music where the same influence is not hard to detect. The fine theme with which Dvorák begins his Symphony 'From the New World' is modal. Much of the work of the Hungarian composers

Bartók and Kodály is modal, for reasons which are explained in Chapter 7. The Finnish composer Sibelius, whose works are frequently evocative of his native land although he hardly ever consciously quoted folk music, derives some part of the austerity of his music from modal sources.

Other composers used modes less deliberately to recreate particular moods and more deliberately to change the inner nature of music itself. Among these Debussy was pre-eminent. For Debussy used many different details from various systems in order to achieve the clarity that he desired.

The aim of the musician is to bring order into the world of sound. Pope Gregory's intention was to bring order into life. At some point the two objectives became the same. But there are always two ways of looking at the one problem. Gregory the Great sought to impose order. Many centuries later Debussy wrote: 'Discipline must be sought in freedom, not in formulas. . . .' Whichever way you look at it, however, the idea of discipline is there. The Gregorian idea in music started out with a strong disciplinarian bias. It never really lost it.

VI

Forty-Eight Preludes and Fugues

Sol-fa name	d	r	m	f	s	l	t	d'
Staff notation								
Alphabetical name	C	D	E	F	G	A	B	C

A S IN literature so in music there is a handful of works of which everyone (whether closely connected with the art or not) should at least be aware. These are the foundation of our experience and our appreciation.

They are also part of the foundation of our form of civilisation, and by knowing them we know a good deal more about ourselves, our traditions, and way of life and thought.

Among the most important of musical compositions two collections of pieces by the great German composer Johann Sebastian Bach take a high place. They are called 'The Well-tempered Clavier' (Books I and II). In each book there are twenty-four 'preludes and fugues'. Each item – that is the prelude and the fugue attached to it – is in a different key. The composition and compilation of these pieces represented a turning-point in the tradition and technique of music.

In the previous chapter we learned something about certain arrangements of sounds which were called modes. Built up step-wise these modes showed the basic sounds – from which musical patterns could be made – that were generally accepted during one period of history. One mode varied from another because each one had its own final-note (also starting note) and because the tones and the half- or semi-tones occurred in one order in one mode and a different order in another.

The greater part of our own musical experience has not been based on the modal system that prevailed once upon a time, but on those scales which still form an important part of the student's piano practice. Very soon in our study of the piano we are taught to play the notes shown at the head of the chapter.

Because the starting-note of this series is that which, for the sake of convenience, is called 'C', this order of notes is known as the scale of C major. Why it has 'major' added to it will be explained shortly. There are tones and half-tones in that scale, the latter having already been shown on page 83.

Now supposing we decide to reproduce that order of tones and half-tones but beginning on a new starting-note. Let us, for example, begin on D. If we use only the white keys we find that we have played the Dorian mode, Ex. 2a on page 83.

That gives us the intervals for the major scale in the wrong places. Turn back to page 90. However, the keyboard has black notes as well as white and by selecting two of the black keys we can successfully reach this conclusion : (Ex. 2.)

Ex.2

The black keys are marked X. By using F *sharp* and C *sharp* instead of F (*natural*) and C (*natural*) we are able to play the notes of the scale of D major, in which the semi- (half-) tones and tones come in the same places as in the scale of C major.

Within an octave on the keyboard there are twelve possible different starting-points, which you can see for yourself. Therefore we can have that number of *major* scales, in all of which the relationship of any one degree to another is the same. This is most easily verified by singing the different major scales to the sol-fa syllables.

There were eight modes in Pope Gregory's time, to which four more were later added – twelve in all. These were replaced by two scales. The one was the *major*, the other the *minor*. The minor scale closely resembles one of the modes in particular. The old so-called Aeolian mode, shown on page 83, lies between *lah* and *lah'*. In the course of time this was modified to – (Ex. 3)

and this became known as a minor scale. When the piano student plays a (melodic) minor scale he finds that he goes up one way and comes down by a slightly modified route – like this : (Ex. 4.)

We see that the minor scale is a little more complicated than the major scale.

As we listen to it we notice that it seems to have a different character from the major scale. This is brought about by the placing of the half- and full-tones, and by the fact that the distance between the key-note and that which lies next but one above it (the third note) is less than in the major scale. It will be seen on page 105 how Bach drew special attention to this difference of interval. In the very simplest terms it has often been felt that the minor is the 'sad' scale and the major the 'cheerful' scale. Just as we can have twelve major scales so may we also have twelve minor scales. Twelve *plus* twelve makes twenty-four. That is where we come in – with Johann Sebastian Bach's twice twenty-four Preludes and Fugues.

From this you will rightly conclude that Bach decided to write a prelude and fugue in each of the possible keys, and that he was so pleased with what he had done that he decided to repeat the exercise. The first set of these pieces were composed in 1722 when Bach worked at the Duke's Court at Cöthen. The second set came in 1744, when he was Director of Music in the city of Leipzig.

But what about the overall title – 'The Well-tempered Clavier'?

Let us look back at the keyboard again. If we play all the twelve notes – white and black – within an octave we hear the sequence given at the beginning of the first chapter as the 'chromatic' scale. Each interval in this scale is a half-tone, so that the distance between any two consecutive notes is the same. But this result can only be arrived at by a certain amount of cheating in tuning the instrument.

If we were to try to build up a twelve-note chromatic scale out of the natural series of harmonics already discussed on page 31 and page 60 we would find that certain of the notes in the *chromatic scale* as shown above would sound out of tune to our ears, which have been conditioned by the tuning of the piano. In effect the difference is so slight that by small adjustments the scale can be conveniently divided into twelve equal parts. But it took a long time to reach this conclusion.

The singer makes his own notes. So too does the string player. If they wish to do so both singers and string players can produce a larger range of intervals than can the pianist or the organist. Part of the fascination of Oriental music in particular lies in the fact that intervals less than half-tones are commonly used.

If a violinist plays (Ex. 5) and then (Ex. 6) the third note of the first group (X) may well be very slightly different from the third note of the second group (X). If, however, you play those two passages on the piano you will use the *same* black key for the third note in each case. In fact, it would be very inconvenient for the keyboard player if this were not possible. The truth is that theoretical considerations must at all times be made to fit into a practical scheme – otherwise many of the things that have become an essential part of music would be impossible.

We are now so accustomed to having things done for us by specialists that we do not always appreciate how all-round people needed to be in earlier times. A composer nowadays is not normally a piano-tuner. But when Bach learned music he had also to learn how to take care of instruments and to be able to tune the keyboard instruments. It was especially important in respect of clavichords and harpsichords, which went very quickly out of tune : they still do and if ever you possess such an instrument it would be as well to discover how to keep it in tune. In so doing you will also improve your skill in precise listening.

Before Bach's day there was uncertainty as to how to tune the scale. After Bach's day on the whole there was not (even though uncertainty about *pitch* remained). The scale adjusted to the principle of twelve equal half-tones was called a tempered scale. Hence the title of the 'well-tempered' clavier.

It is interesting at this point to recall how some people wanted the best of both worlds. A famous German musician and writer, Michael Praetorius, organist at Wolfenbüttel near Brunswick, once visited an organist in Prague in the early seventeenth century. He found that this organist possessed a harpsichord which had nineteen notes to each octave in order to accommodate different tunings. One of the pianos made by Zumpe (see Chapter 2) had extra keys fitted, so that the performer could play in the 'untempered' and also in the 'tempered' scale. And some organs in England were preserved with a pre-Bach tuning until well into the nineteenth century. It is curious that the famous organist, Samuel Sebastian Wesley, a great enthusiast for Bach's music, actually preferred an older form of tuning. The objections against trying to contain different tunings on a keyboard instrument were on the whole practical.

The keyboard as we now know it, and as it has been for a long time, is convenient to the hand. It is worth noting that Bach, the great teacher, thought out every problem in a practical way, and that he examined carefully the relationship between hand and keyboard. He was said to have been the first teacher to advocate the use of the thumb in playing.

You may wonder what all the fuss over tuning was about anyway. You may begin to find out by listening to music of different periods. If you listen to a keyboard piece of the seventeenth century – say by the Englishman John Bull or by his Dutch friend Jan Sweelinck you will find that while the melodic tones may be rich, and the combination of melodic lines with patterns of counterpoint fascinating, the chords or harmonies are relatively simple. If you then turn to a keyboard piece by Henry Purcell you will feel that the harmonies are more varied. When you come to Bach they are often more varied still. It will be noticed that within a piece by Bach there are more frequent shifts of tonal centre – or changes of key.

This gave a new dimension to music. But it was one that could hardly be explored until the common-sense adjustment to tuning made by the system of equal temperament was adopted. We have previously seen that what appears as a 'great idea' in music is due to a desire for simplification and for orderliness. That was born of the Schoenbergian reform, and also of the Gregorian system. Bach, who had a tidy mind, saw that if there was uniformity in the matter of tuning then many new fields could be opened up for exploration. And so it turned out.

It is only fair to say that there were many before Bach's day who had the same general idea.

During the sixteenth century there lived in Venice a famous musician and theorist named Gioseffe Zarlino, who was one of the teachers of Vincenzo Galilei, an influential member of the early Florentine school of opera. In the course of their discussions (which aroused a certain amount of bad temper!) Zarlino and Galilei spent much time talking about the subject of tuning. Zarlino took Galilei's favourite instrument, the lute, and showed how convenient it would be if the octave were divided into twelve equal semi-tones. In one of his works Zarlino wrote down the principles on which equal temperament could be built. A Spanish composer, Francesco Salinas, also advocated a system of equal temperament, which the famous German organist, Johann Kerll, who died when Bach was a boy of eight, composed a work on a 'ground bass' (a repeated theme as in the passacaglia) that passed through all the keys.

The feeling for a wider harmonic range can be appreciated from some of the bass parts which composers used during the Baroque period for the purpose of 'ground bass' pieces. Here is an example of a straightforward ground bass, the foundation of a song by Henry Purcell. (Ex. 7.) Here is a ground bass to be

Ex. 7

O   so-li-tude, my   sweet - - est choice!

Voice

Harpsichord

etc.

Ex.8

Orchestra

found in one of Bach's Church Cantatas (Ex. 8). This bass shows part of the 'chromatic' scale and is one which was used by many composers. The same bass lies below the 'Crucifixion' section of the *Mass in B Minor*. It occurs in another Church Cantata (No. 78). It is similar to the bass part of Purcell's 'When I am laid in earth' (*Dido and Aeneas*). And it may be found in numerous keyboard pieces by other composers of that period. In each case when we have heard one note we ask ourselves where we go next. In music as chromatic as the second example we don't know. We may think we know; but the composer, able to go in more than one direction if he chooses, will often surprise us.

Now Bach was only interested in theories insofar as they enabled him to write more interesting music. He was, first and foremost, a practical musician. Before he was a composer he was a performer – a violinist, a harpsichordist, a clavichordist, an organist. And he was, of course, a teacher. He was a good teacher as we know from the quality of his pupils. He wrote keyboard music to play himself, or to provide suitable studies for his pupils. He realised, however, that all music needed a special quality if it was to be worth the name of music. It should stir the imagination, and the emotions. There is not one among the Forty-eight Preludes and Fugues that does not do this.

In the course of this book the word freedom has occurred a number of times. The idea of freedom is precious to all men, but most have only a vague and general conception of its meaning. The artist, however, must think a great deal about its meaning.

He must think on two levels. First, there is the necessity to have freedom to create. Often this is a hardly won freedom. Bach, for example, was always busy in countless ways and although he was expected by his employers to compose music he had many duties to perform before he could begin. Fortunately he lived in a society which accepted the creative function of the artist as it accepted the creative function of the craftsman. Indeed the composer of that period, especially in Germany, was regarded as a craftsman; and he regarded himself as such.

But when a composer sits down at his table with his manuscript before him he must look again at the question of freedom. In theory he can make whatever music he wishes to make. In practice no composer can ever do quite that. His freedom is limited by his personality: this explains why the music of Bach sounds different in many ways from that of his contemporaries, Handel and Telemann. His freedom is limited by his training, for the habits imposed by stern teachers (and teachers of those days were strict) endure. His freedom is limited by environment, so that without opportunity to write operas Bach composed nothing in this field. Above all his freedom is limited by the desire for order that is the distinguishing mark of the great artist.

We sometimes think that progress (as we perhaps mistakenly call it) in art comes because barriers are broken down. In one sense this is true. In another it is not. When some barriers are destroyed others are put up, but not always in the same place. This is what we discovered in the first chapter. Schoenberg gave a greater sense of freedom to composers of the twentieth century by dismantling the already rather broken-down fences of the nineteenth century; but he made it quite clear that the idea of discipline still stood firm.

Bach lived in an age of change. He saw that the style of music practised by the younger generation – which included his own talented sons – was of a different order. The new music of the 1720's and 1730's was lighter, gayer, more tinged with sentiment. There were those who thought that Bach himself was out-of-date, and they said so. Bach was the last man in the world to change his convictions simply to bring himself in line with fashion. If he had done so he would have lost his freedom. This is an important point for us, who live in an age when the force of fashion is much greater, to bear in mind.

The music of Bach is characterised by its linear character. That is to say, we are always aware of the movement of many strands of melody at the same time. If we look for a 'tune', just like that, we may be disappointed. Not always – but often. The reason for this is that for hundreds of years before Bach's time the most important musical works had been constructed on the principle of equality of opportunity for each participant. For good reasons the basis of European art-music (as distinct from folk-music) was the vocal ensemble. A vocal ensemble contained high voices and low voices, often conveniently described as soprano (or treble), alto, tenor, and bass. This division of registers carried on with instrumental music.

Musical design is rooted more in common-sense than in 'inspiration'. Because of this the idea of theme and variations (where the composer has a musical idea to start with) is to be found in all phases of musical development. In the previous chapter it was shown that Gregorian melodies became part of the structure of religious worship. Because of this – for church music dominated all music for centuries – these melodies became the basis not only of tradition but also of experiment in composition.

In the masses and motets which grew out of the Gregorian tradition familiar melodies, or parts of such melodies, were constant features. But increasingly these melodia ideas served as spurs to invention.

The composer gives a traditional theme to one singer (or group of singers). This we may conveniently term the *subject*. Above it, or below it, he may place another melody for another singer, or group. The second melody running against, or counter to, the first, is a *counter-subject*. This second melody contrasts with the first, but is bound to it in the sense that it must somehow appear to 'fit in'. This way of composing music, however, has its limitations. As you may have found out when singing or playing a *descant* (which is what the counter-subject described above is) the period of the music is determined by the length of the main melody. Arrived at the end of that the music stops.

The composer may, on the other hand, give a fragment of melody to one voice (part). Having let it out he may then give the same fragment to a second voice. If he does this, because the second voice may lie within a different register, the second statement may very well be at a different pitch. The principle may be followed up, until three, four . . . seven, eight . . . eleven, twelve, parts are involved in the music.

It was on such a principle – rooted in the need for basing musical expression on a *single* idea, accommodated to a group of performers each of whom was an individual – that the large works of the later Middle Ages and the early Renaissance were built. The principle was later described sometimes as Gothic by those who saw some similarity of idea between the works of musicians on one hand and architects on the other. One writer, the Englishman Charles Burney, referred to the fugues of Bach as Gothic. In this case he was trying to be superior, pointing out how old-fashioned Bach was in his outlook.

The practice of melodic imitation in this manner gave the forms of canon and round and the *method* of fugue. A canon and a round are strict, as you may notice by taking part in the performance of such. A fugue is much more free, although it will always sound disciplined because of the controlling effect of the principal subject matter.

Fugal method was derived from the nature of vocal ensemble music. When instruments grew in esteem and composers had opportunity to compose for keyboard instruments or for ensembles they transferred the well-tried structural principles of vocal music. In the seventeenth century there was a marvellously exciting cross-over of techniques. The fugal pattern so long established in singing gave rise to instrumental works of great power and originality. Among the most rewarding instrumental works of the age were the string fantasias of English composers, the most mature, perhaps being those of Matthew Locke and Henry Purcell, and the keyboard fugues of Girolamo Frescobaldi, Dietrich Buxtehude, and Johann Pachelbel.

Bach was a diligent student of music. He knew that he could only perfect his own techniques by analysing those of others. Schoenberg went deep into the styles of Brahms and Wagner, the significant composers of his youth. Similarly Bach examined the works of Pachelbel. He had a particular reason for doing so. Pachelbel had once lived in Eisenach where Bach was born, and, a friend of the family, he was godfather to one of Bach's sisters.

When he was a young man Bach once walked all the way from Thuringia to the Baltic sea port of Lübeck where Buxtehude was organist of St Mary's Church in order to hear that great man's music. At another time he made a fair copy of a collection of pieces by Frescobaldi. By these exercises he was living not in the past but the present.

Fugue developed within a church setting. It therefore acquired associations. To this day composers use fugal method of design when they wish to suggest the idea of solemnity. There is an example in the third movement of the Fourth Symphony of the American composer Charles Ives. When the great organists of the seventeenth century took over fugal patterns and adapted them to the nature of their instrument the sense of association strengthened. Bach composed many fugues – for he was brought up to accept this as a regular form of design. A large proportion of his fugues lie within his works for church use. The fugues which he wrote for organ, however, have very little in the way of narrowly religious meaning. In character they vary greatly.

This, however, they have in common : that in them Bach was exploring the resources of music in order to give expression to his views on the world, and on life in general. We may say this not because he made statements that can be found in any form of words, but because there is such a variety of musical ideas expressed and discussed. It is a sound rule that if you want to appreciate one piece of music you should listen to two, or three, or – forty-eight. By this means you discover the extent of a composer's outlook by the diversity of his musical ideas.

We have seen that the first set of the 'Forty-eight' was composed at Cöthen in 1722. Behind it lay the principle of equal temperament in tuning. But there was another principle – one to Bach that was of greater importance. His son Wilhelm Friedemann was now twelve years old. It was time he was getting to grips with more difficult keyboard pieces. When the second part of the 'Forty-eight' was composed in 1744 Johann Christoph, the eldest surviving son of Bach's second marriage, was also coming up to twelve years of age. Believing that the good teacher adjusted his teaching to the individual needs of his pupils Bach wrote many exercises and extended musical works for them. He did his pupils the honour of believing that their interests were in tune with his own, and he never wrote down to them. It was hard work being taught by Bach, for much was expected, but how stimulating it was.

This is evident from the 'Forty-eight'. As we listen to them, or better still, play through them, we find that each shows a different aspect of music. We may say that each has a different character. Because we speak in this way of 'character' we relate the music to the world as we experience it in everyday life. We persuade ourselves therefore that the music is 'about' whatever we wish to think it is about. Bach had no such 'programme' ideas – at least if he had we do not know what they were – but there is no reason why we should not do so if this ensures that the music becomes part of our life by these means.

There is no doubt, however, that Bach was coming to meet us by employing all the possible keys in order to extend the power of expression of music. This may be shown by the opening bars of two fugues, Nos. 9 (in E major) and 12 (in F minor) from the first book. (Ex. 9 and Ex. 10.)

In the first example the mood is almost casual, and carefree. In the second, which has a sterner rhythm, there appears to be more effort in the way in which the notes of subject, countersubject, and *answer*, establish themselves. The subject of the Fugue in F minor seems mid-way to go far away from the key. The shape of this melody, only credible with an equal temperament tuning, seems to look forward to the attitude of some melodic patterns that have come to us since Schoenberg. The character of each subject dictates the manner of development, so that there is a consistent individuality in each piece. It also

reaches back to the respective preludes, as the opening bars again
suggest. (Ex. 11 and Ex. 12.) If Exs. 10 and 12 are compared
with Ex. 8 above it will be seen that all three are in the same
key of F minor and it may also be felt that this gives a common
atmosphere, or mood. If the two preludes are compared, the
contrast between a major and a minor key is strongly marked.
It happens that the bar in E major is quite similar in shape to
that in F minor (particularly look at the left hand parts). Both
begin over a sustained note in the bass. But each prelude appears
to be in feeling quite unrelated to the other.

   Bach was a modest man so far as his compositions were concerned. He understood that there were other composers, whom
he knew, who were much more fashionable – and much more
successful. Handel, from all accounts, was doing very well for
himself – in England. Telemann was rushing about all over
Europe turning out concertos and suites and operas and church
music without much trouble and to great applause. Bach was
firmly anchored in a provincial part of Germany. Perhaps that
was his safeguard. He was in the position of not having to study
the likes and dislikes of the public so much as his more illustrious
friends.

'The Forty-eight' is one of the great anthologies of music. Bach simply headed it in this way :

'The Well-tuned Clavier, or, Preludes and Fugues in all the tones and half-tones, alike with the major third (or *d, t, m*) and with the minor third (or *r, m, f*) : for the use of young musicians who are eager to learn, and also as a pastime for those who are already capable of this kind of music. . . .'

Bach's sons were introduced to these pieces at about the age of twelve. At the same age Beethoven first began to play them. His teacher in the Rhineland city of Bonn was Christian Neefe who had been a student in Leipzig. Beethoven was ever grateful to his teacher that he had come to this music so early in life. The influence of Bach was very strong. Beethoven brought the fugal impulse into many of his works and the 'Great Fugue' in B flat (Op. 133) is, perhaps, the best memorial to Bach created by Beethoven. This fugue was intended to conclude a string quartet (both Haydn and Mozart ended string quartets with fugal movements), but being so large was left to stand by itself. It may often be heard arranged for string orchestra.

It was more than half a century before 'The Forty-eight' was published. In the years intervening between composition and publication manuscript copies were made. In 1800 one publisher in Zürich, Switzerland, and another in Bonn published editions. Some years later the English musician Samuel Wesley, inspired by copies shown to him by German friends, and helped by Charles Horn, a German organist living in England, issued the first English edition. Since then no young musician has been considered properly educated without a first-hand acquaintance with 'The Forty-eight'.

There is the danger that the too great enthusiasm of the teacher and the theorist may take away the edge of your appreciation of these, and other works, by Bach. It is not how they are made that's important – even though this is interesting – but what they are all about. Listen to, or play, them and you will find out.

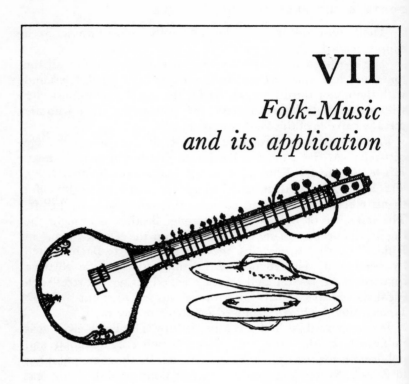

VII

*Folk-Music
and its application*

IN WHAT are termed the 'advanced' countries folk-music
has become a kind of sacred cow. The teacher in the school
dutifully begins a lesson with – 'Today we are going to learn
a folk-song. It is very beautiful. . . .' The musical scholar rushes
round in circles arguing about the proper method of collecting
folk-music, the way to put it down on paper, the style of interpretation, the meaning (often hidden) of the words, and so on. And
there is a new kind of pop-singer who pulls the once free shapes
of folk-melodies into line with current rhythmic patterns and
props them up against a background of guitar strumming. This

may be very beguiling in its own way, but it is a long way from folk-song proper.

All of this tells us that the art of folk-music in such countries is dead. Its cult is a form of escape from an age or a society in which there is little opportunity for creative activity on the part of the majority; a recognition of the fact that the passing of folk-music as a living art has left a gap.

Folk-music within its proper tradition and environment in fact is one obvious sign of man's creative nature. It is one of the few forms of art that exists to a high degree for its own sake.

Now if folk-music is dead in the 'advanced' societies it is as yet far from dead in the 'under-developed' regions of the world. If we wish to find out what folk-music is really like – or what it means to people – we must travel to distant villages in. Asia, or India, or Africa. If we are lucky enough to be able to do this we find ourselves in a quite new world of music : one that makes us think all over again about our own music and its purpose.

Left by ourselves we jump to too many conclusions : that *our* form of music is of supreme importance; that *our*, European, or American, composers are the greatest masters not only so far as our own societies are concerned but also for those who have never heard of them ! If, however, we forget our prejudices and our pride and try to put aside what *we* consider to be the foundation of musical experience, and listen to folk-music as practised in faraway places, we realise that there is a wide field of thrilling and beautiful music to be explored. And we can learn much from it.

In Africa and Asia there are hundreds and hundreds of different languages and dialects. Each language and each dialect, binding together a group of people, has its own form of music. Folk-song grows out of speech and reflects its pitch-changes and rhythms. This is because folk-song originally was hardly more than a more intense form of speaking. A heightening of speech may sometimes be heard in church where the priest neither

speaks nor sings but *intones*. Intonation, intended to emphasize
important statements, as we have seen, has come into our musical
tradition by way of Gregorian plainsong.

In certain African languages the meaning of a word alters
according to variation of the pitch of its syllables. This means
that when using such a language the speaker and his listeners
must listen with musical ears. This, of course, they do unconsciously. In regard to European languages we must also
learn to think in a musical way – of the tone colours of syllables,
and, above all, of the stresses and accents within words and
phrases. But the gap between the European languages and the
music of their cultures is much greater than in the other societies,
largely because of the independent development of instrumental
forms of music.

The European or American naturally thinks of the *art* of
music. The African, or Asian, or Indian, in his village does not
know that music is an art. He does not stop to think. He absorbs
the musical expression of his people without question.

A living folk-music is an essential part of life. Thus the tribal
community celebrates betrothals, marriages and births, sounds
the summons when danger threatens, accompanies the sowing
of the land and the reaping of the harvest, and mourns the
deaths of its members, with music, with song, with dance, with
instrumental music, and with music and action brought together
into a kind of folk-opera.

Folk-music is rich, untidy, never held in one place by theories,
ever absorbing new ideas. In short it expands and grows at a
rate that we would think rather alarming within the field of
'art music'.

One may hear songs sung in parts : the harmonies are not our
harmonies. Strangely – or perhaps not strangely – the harmonies
that are to be discovered in Western Africa are those which were
to a large extent used in European music anything up to a
thousand years ago. Songs are often accompanied – by drums

and a variety of percussion instruments, by flutes made from bamboo, by raft zithers, by thumb-pianos, by xylophones made from banana wood. These instruments accompany dances and often are played independently.

It is wrong even to think of music of this kind as 'primitive'. The way in which singers decorate and enlarge on familiar melodies is beyond our powers; the rhythmic complexity of the instrumental performances is far removed from the simplicities of your book of piano pieces. Above all, expression is not an addition to note-patterns that have been carefully learned. It is felt as a part of the music that is there at its birth.

Folk-music has been zealously preserved for many hundreds of years in some communities. In many cases those who have done most to keep it alive are those who were formerly spoken of as bards, or minstrels : people with a special aptitude. In some cases musical cultures of the greatest interest have developed as a result of the devoted studies of the minstrels (by whatever name they may be known).

Indian instrumental music is known to many of us through the great artistry of the world-famous sitar player Ravi Shankar.

The music of India, which has been maintained for nearly two thousand years, is primarily melodic. It is based on traditional *ragas* (types of scales which often employ smaller intervals than our half-tone) and *talas* (subtle rhythmic formulas). Using the *ragas* and *talas* as guiding principles the instrumentalist improvises – often for very long periods.

'The most fascinating aspect of Indian music', says Yehudi Menuhin, 'is the awareness of the harmony between Man and Nature, each acting and reacting on the other, and hence each *raga* is associated, according to its mood, with a particular time of the day or night, or with a season.' Speaking further of Indian music, Menuhin says, 'Perhaps this music has come to us just in time to redeem our moribund melody.'

In the first chapter we learned how one great musician of the twentieth century tried to remove the dead-weight of European musical conventions. While Schoenberg looked inward, seeking to *think* new ways of composition, other composers looked outward. The French composer Claude Debussy (1862–1918) was entranced by the African and Asian music that was performed at an exhibition in Paris in 1889, and deeply interested in the studies of Chinese music made by his friend Louis Laloy. Debussy did much to liberate music from the so-called 'classical' theories, and his appreciation of the qualities of pure sound opened a new era in the colour principles of music. A good example of Debussy's approach is a piece called *Syrinx*, of which the closing bars are given. (Ex. 1.)

This (incidental music for a play) was composed for a single unaccompanied flute. As you hear it you must, as in the case of Indian music, *forget* that you have been told, perhaps, is 'correct'. This is music which sounds as though it is being freely improvised. In the last three bars the melody falls a tone at a time. Thus we hear the effect of the *whole-tone* scale which Debussy often used.

Another French composer, of our own day, Oliver Messaien, also frequently employs unaccompanied melody. He studied the styles of Indian music and tried to bring them into European music. Messaien has something in common with the Indian masters. Much of his music is inspired by bird-song and he once asked: 'What is there left but to rediscover the true forgotten

FOLK-MUSIC AND ITS APPLICATION   III

face of music somewhere in the woods, in the fields, in the
mountains, by the sea, among the birds?' He added: 'There, for
me, is the home of music.'

So far as African rhythms and instruments are concerned the
German composer Carl Orff has applied some of their principles
not only to his own compositions but also to music-teaching in
schools. Those who are acquainted with Orff's *Music for
Children* will know what exciting ideas he has put before teacher
and pupils alike.

In America where there was not, as in European countries,
one recognisable form of national music composers reached out
in all directions to find the most exciting and expressive ideas.
Henry Gilbert (1868–1928), a pupil of Macdowell, was a pioneer
in introducing negro music into concert pieces. His *The Dance
in Place Congo* was the best-known of his orchestral works.
Arthur Farwell (1872–1952) who was trained as an engineer at
the Massachusetts Institute of Technology, studied music in
Europe and found himself in revolt against the regular methods
and vocabulary of composition, which did not seem to offer
much to one who wished the music of his own country to stem
from national sources. Farwell introduced into his works melodies
of the American Indians, and also melodic patterns derived from
the Oriental scales which he had studied in detail. In his later
works, *Curlew River* and *The Burning Fiery Furnace*, Benjamin
Britten has borrowed ideas from the traditional drama-with-music
of Japan.

It takes a great musician to unite aspects of idoms so far apart
as the western and the oriental. Sometimes a lesser musician
turns away from what is familiar to him and tries to cultivate an
unusual style as a gesture of despair. He who can work from
what is truly living in his own environment is in the happiest
condition.

This is where we may with profit look at the musical tradition
of Hungary, which has been made familiar to the world at large

by two great composers, Béla Bartók (1881–1945) and Zoltán
Kodály (1882–1967). There are some who would claim the former as the greatest composer of the twentieth century. Of the latter
it may be said that not only was he a great composer but also,
perhaps, the most influential teacher (not only of music) of the age.

Bartók and Kodály each based his life's work on the foundation of the music of the Hungarian people – the folk-music that
was still a living force when they were students in the early years
of the twentieth century.

When it is practised as a part of a social routine folk-music
is the most alive of all forms of music. It springs directly from
life – to the outsider it marvellously reflects the life of a group
of people; it is always in a state of change because, although the
main structure is rooted in tradition, it takes new forms according to the talent for improvisation of the performer. Since
folk-music is never written down as it exists in its natural setting
but is transmitted aurally it is, so to speak, always 'modern'. It
has a positive character, for it symbolises the will of a society,
which it also helps to maintain and to inspire.

In times of stress people – through their musicians – frequently
turn to folk-music, almost as though it really had the magical
powers sometimes attributed to it.

In many countries, in the late nineteenth and early twentieth
centuries, folk-music played its part in the fight for freedom from
foreign domination. One of these countries was Hungary.

When we speak of the domination of one country by another
we recognise that this is likely to show in two ways. There is
political domination – which is easy to recognise; there is cultural
domination, which is not always so easy to appreciate. Very
often the two are joined together, for when one strong country
controls another that is weaker it usually assumes that it has the
right to impose its 'way of life'. The 'way of life' is what otherwise is termed culture, and of this music is an important part.

To go away from the present, where there are many examples

to think about, there may be instanced the long years of control of Ireland by the English. During these years Irish national culture – which had an old and brilliant tradition – was all but put out of existence. At any rate so far as the influential public was concerned.

Hungary, which also had a glorious and rich artistic history up to the time of the Renaissance, was under the rule of foreign powers for more than four hundred years. During the most important era of musical development – the age of 'classical' music – the country was governed from Vienna, as part of the Austrian Empire. For obvious reasons the people of importance in the Hungarian towns – especially in Budapest, the capital – behaved more like Viennese than Hungarians and the culture of Vienna set the standard. The language of the people of the towns was German. The programmes of concerts contained only the works (great though many of them were) that were fashionable among the Viennese aristocracy. Young artists learned to think, and to create, according to the current German fashion.

One of the great classical composers, Joseph Haydn, was of Magyar stock. He used an international language of music – indeed he helped to make the language of music international. From time to time, however, we become aware of his origins. This is shown by the reference on page 50. But what Haydn was doing in this case was not to produce a Hungarian work, but to flavour his style with Hungarian idioms, which helped to give his music more character and to make it more expressive. Haydn, although devoted to the countryside in which he was born and where he always had many friends and relatives to visit, did not think as a 'nationalist'. A simple man, he accepted life as it was; and under the patronage of the Esterházys it was more comfortable than uncomfortable.

A hundred years later a Hungarian did not accept life as it was. During the nineteenth century there had been great political unrest, as in the whole of Europe, and the bravest of the

Hungarians had fought for independence. In Haydn's day the language of music was fresh and invigorating. At the end of the Romantic movement, which he had also helped to create, the language of music was artificial and stuffy (save in the hands of a few men of vision). Now was the time to look for a new language. We now approach the crisis in music arrived at from a different direction in the first chapter.

Zoltán Kodály was born in a village. He knew the folk-customs of the peasants at first hand. He understood that they were more meaningful than much of the art music that was practised. Above all he saw the character that the folk-songs carried simply through the fact that they were in the Hungarian language. More than this Kodály – as he wrote fifty years later – saw that as the singing of folk-song gave strength and unity to a society so there was a great chance of bringing together people of different countries through the medium of singing.

Like the philosophers of earlier times Kodály felt that music could exert a moral influence, that it could help to improve society :

'If', he wrote, 'in those far-off days we had been taught what I try to teach . . . life would have been very different in our little country. It is left with you who use this book to show that while singing in itself is good the real reward comes to those who sing, and feel, and think, with others. This is what harmony means.

'We must look forward to the time when all people in all lands are brought together through singing, and there is a universal harmony.'

As a student Kodály learned the history of his country and of its language. But he was intent on being a composer. And here there was a problem. As we have already seen a young composer at the beginning of the century had before him the example of Brahms and Wagner. To become a composer at all it was, as Schoenberg discovered, essential to start on familiar ground.

Kodály's early works owed much to the classical tradition. Most of all in the matter of clarity of form. Among the works which won high praise in the first decade of the twentieth century were a fine string quartet (Op. 2) and a sonata for 'cello and piano. There were also some choral arrangements of Hungarian folk-songs. The chamber music already reflected ideas that belonged to the folk-music tradition. Melodic patterns in which the intervals of 5th $(d - s)$ and 4th $(s - d)$ were common, and flexibility of rhythm, shown in unaccustomed changes of time-signature, distinguished the idiom. At the same time there was, and there has remained, a warmth in the harmonic texture and in the handling of piano figures, that stemmed from the Romantic climate of the music Kodály was accustomed to play at home in his youth.

When Kodály was becoming established as a composer two musical traditions existed side by side in his country : the proud and humane tradition of European music – which was represented by the greatest of composers from Bach to Brahms and not to be thought of as 'national' except by fervid nationalists – and the rich, exciting, lively tradition of folk-music. Kodály loved both traditions, and appreciated that the two should live together. As a scholar he pursued his researches into folk-music and built up a rich store of Hungarian music. In the course of time he taught many pupils and inspired them with his ideals, so that by now the techniques of Hungarian musical scholars in the sphere of folk-music research are unsurpassed anywhere in the world. Much of the work has been conducted under the auspices of the Hungarian Academy of Sciences. By the side of musical research there have been remarkable achievements in other branches of folk-lore.

It is admirable to collect the evidence of man's natural creative skills that folk-art provides. But this art only becomes valuable when it is absorbed, as it were, into the blood-stream to stimulate a renewed faith. There were, as has been seen, many

composers of the nineteenth century who paid lip-service to
folk-art. But merely sticking labels in the form of national tunes
on to musical structures signifies little.

The composer who believes in his mission (whatever the kind
of music he composes) must live within a medium of expression
which is to be experienced as a whole. This means knowing the
way of life which gives rise to a folk-art from the outside. In
painting we have the example of Paul Gauguin, the great
French artist who forsook Paris and went to live in the South
Seas in order to find out a fresh relationship between people
and art.

Kodály discovered how to develop the style he wished to
achieve by seeing music as a great constructive force in society.
He understood most of all the relationship between word and
melody. Turning to the classical lyrical poets of Hungary he
composed songs that reflected the rhythm and the colour of the
Magyar language and which gained in intensity and meaning
from the emotional quality of their accompaniments.

In 1923, however, there came an opportunity to reach a
wider audience than was possible through the medium of solo
songs. Budapest, the Hungarian capital, is a federation of two
ancient towns lying on opposite banks of the Danube. The one
was Buda, the other was Pest. In 1923 celebrations in honour
of the jubilee of their federation were held. Kodály was commissioned to compose a work. He chose a famous poem, a para-
phrase of a psalm, written by a Hungarian patriot-poet in the
sixteenth century. The poem is tragic, passionate, full of hope.
Kodály understood that it expressed the feelings of Hungarians
not only in the sixteenth but also in the twentieth century. His
setting, for soloists, choir and orchestra, contains all the elements
that distinguish the poetry. In rhythm and in melodic outline it
enshrines much that is to be found in Hungarian folk-music. But
the orchestral writing, as assured as that of any modern work,
embraces many of the conventions that have no narrow and
limited meaning.

The character of the *Psalmus Hungaricus* is distinctive, not because it is Hungarian but because it is created by a Hungarian. A great composer always stands by himself; yet he understands his responsibility to his people. In this sense the great composer, aware of the power he is capable of exercising, is in the situation of the bard of former times.

The *Psalmus Hungaricus* enhanced the composer's reputation. It was acclaimed not only in Hungary but throughout Europe. But more important was the fact that at home Kodály, who had striven so hard and so long and against considerable opposition, was now regarded not only as a musician but as a citizen of importance. Through his musical works he has continued across the years to demonstrate how a musician can, on the one hand, express, and on the other, influence national thought.

Elsewhere in this book the contrast between tragedy and comedy is dealt with. An artist of the stature of Kodály deals with both. The *Psalmus Hungaricus* is a noble and tragic work. The folk-opera *Háry János*, in contrast, is noble and comic. It is, perhaps, the one truly comic opera of the twentieth century. Composed in 1929 it tell the story of a legendary and fantastic character, Háry János, who accomplished many improbable and valiant deeds – but only in his imagination. Like Till Eulenspiegel and Don Quixote and Jaroslav Hasek's 'Good Soldier Schweik', Háry represents some part of each one of us. The manner in which Kodály illustrates his character by the clever use and arrangement of folk-tunes not only shows aspects of personality in simple and understandable musical language but also gives a particular insight into the expressive power of folk-music. This is also true of the most famous of ballad-operas – *The Beggar's Opera* (see page 177f.)

If opportunities of seeing the opera *Háry János* are rather scarce outside Hungary the orchestral suite based on it is frequently performed. In this one appreciates the wholeness of the musical style, the fact that melody, harmony, rhythm, and orchestration belong together, the one helping the other. The outstanding feature of this music to a non-Hungarian ear is the rhythm.

The vitality of Kodály's rhythmic attitude may be appreciated on two fronts. As already stated his vocal music is rhythmically alive because it springs from the language. His instrumental music is inspired also by song-music – as in the case of the *Peacock Variations* for orchestra. But it is also inspired by a sense of dance. So we may live inside the orchestral *Dances from Marroszék* and *Dances from Galánta,* both of which have been arranged as ballets, and the *Kálló Folk Dances,* which are for chorus and orchestra.

In the works detailed above we recognise Kodály as a familiar figure in the world repertoire of music. His music there exists not because it is Hungarian but because it is music of a distinctive and high quality that adds to the general experience of music. The same may be said of the music that he has composed for the church. Here the outstanding words are the *Te Deum* composed in 1936 in commemoration of the recapture of the city of Buda in 1686, and the *Missa Brevis (Short Mass)* composed during the last days of the Second World War. In these works the finest standards of Renaissance and Classical choral music are revealed in a new environment. Both works, like the *Psalmus Hungaricus,* are as thrilling to sing as they are to hear.

From what has been said it should be clear that Kodály's greatness rests on his belief that the union of the two words 'folk' and 'music' to him means something special. You may have heard 'folk-music' explained as 'music for the people'.

Which people? Kodály answered that question by indicating that he composed (as far as is humanly possible) for *all* and not merely *some* people. But he never assumed that music should be doled out as soup used to be served by self-conscious do-gooders to the 'poor'. He realised that a love of music, and an understanding of life through music, can only come from active participation. Folk-music, after all, was less something to be listened to than to be done.

Now folk-music lingered on as a living force into the twentieth century, not least of all in Hungary. But the future of music does not lie with folk-music as such. For this the changes in the pattern of general living brought about by political, social and technical development, are responsible. We may not go back behind these changes to a former state – which in any case is often highly idealised and even falsified. This is why those who try to promote an interest in folk-music in the wrong way are barking up the wrong tree.

In modern times choral music has taken over some of the properties of folk-music. Choral music indeed has often become a department of folk-art. This is shown by the way in which Welsh people throughout the world so frequently display their identity and proclaim their pride in their nation by spontaneous singing together. Choral music was written into the Hungarian tradition long ago, for a famous choir was formed at the college in Debrecen more than two hundred years ago. This choir, with music specially written for it, helped to popularise choral singing and also to inspire a pride in native music.

In 1929 many bodies of amateur singers met at Debrecen to take part in a festival of music. The number of singers taking part was 10,000. Kodály realised what a great force for musical progress such a body could be. He devoted much of his time and talent, therefore, to the arrangement of folk-songs and to the composition of new works. Among his famous works for unaccompanied voices are the *Mátra Pictures*, and *Jesus and the Traders*, both highly dramatic.

It is taken for granted that orchestral musicians must be able to read music at sight. It is not so frequently allowed that choral singers should be equally competent. Kodály always understood that while musical appreciation depends on feeling it also depends on knowledge. Choral singers should be musically literate. To achieve this then something was required in the field of education.

When the *Psalmus Hungaricus* was first performed the chorus was augmented by a boys' choir. The composer was amazed at what these boys could achieve. On visits to England he was also impressed by the musical ability of the children he heard. He determined to ensure that every Hungarian child should be able to learn music.

Forty years ago there were few capable teachers. The music that was taught was of poor quality. Ability to read at sight was almost non-existent. Across the years Kodály has composed books of sight-reading and vocal exercises – which differ from many such compilations in being truly musical. He has written many articles and delivered many lectures on musical education. He has been responsible for the institution by the government of his country of primary and secondary schools to which children gifted in music may be sent for an education in which music plays a prominent part.

The foundation of this education is unaccompanied singing, and particularly of folk-music. On this foundation a whole experience of music is built – music that is understood from the inside. The influence inside Hungary is very great, but it is also considerable in other parts of the world. For the methods applied by Kodály, his pupils, and disciples, are also being adopted in other countries. Especially in Britain, Canada and the United States.

'We must look forward to the time when all people in all lands are brought together through singing.'

That is the ideal which has grown from one great idea. The idea lies not in words, but in music.

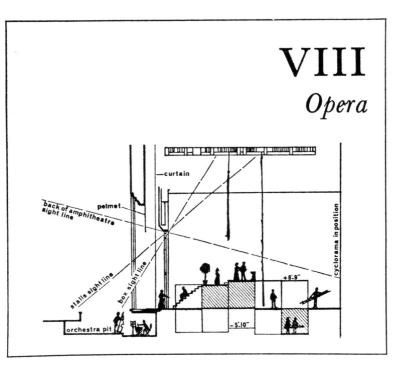

VIII

Opera

The following labels appear on the illustration: curtain, pelmet, back of amphitheatre sight line, cyclorama in position, stalls sight line, box sight line, orchestra pit, +8'-9", -5'-10"

WHEN we go to the opera we use our eyes as well as our ears. We see singers who can act (or actors who can sing), and scenery. The acting and the scenery are an important part of the explanation of the story, or plot, that is the foundation of an opera. The musical part of an opera includes words-set-to-music and, in all but a very few cases, passages of purely instrumental music. This instrumental music, however, is never really independent; for it too must help to add

The illustration above is a sectional elevation of the stage of Covent Garden, showing lifts and sight lines. The shaded areas show three lifts used to their limits above and below the stage.

121

to, or explain, the meaning of the story. At this point it should be said that a story – any story – that holds our interest does so on two levels. We follow the actions of a plot, and in many cases are curious until we see how these work towards a conclusion. At the same time we find ourselves in sympathy with the hero, or the heroine, or the villain – or anyone else. Our feelings and emotions are then involved. Now words can describe actions, but they are less effective in telling us about emotion. Music, on the other hand, is able to do this : this explains why instrumental music has increasingly played an important rôle in opera.

Opera is a complicated but fascinating form of art. On the surface it resembles a play. Many operas indeed have a play as starting-point. For instance, the comedies and tragedies of Shakespeare have inspired a large number of opera-composers. One may ask (and some people do) : why turn a perfectly good play into something else? There are two answers. First, another medium may show aspects of a play that might otherwise be missed. This we may appreciate if we remember some of the best films based on Shakespeare. Second, ideas which are within a play may be deepened if they are given additional expression. It was Pierre de Beaumarchais, the French dramatist, who made a play about 'The Barber of Seville'. And a very good play it was, full of wit and satirical humour. But it was Mozart who made the story universally known through his opera *The Marriage of Figaro*. In this opera Mozart's melodies are not only delightful in themselves but also capture and clearly present the contrasted characters of the story.

We know that music affects our feelings or emotions. A great opera composer knows this and his aim is to invent the right music for the right moment. This is what is meant when the word 'timing' is used in respect of dramatic music. By precise timing the scenes and actions of an opera story come to life, seeming to be real.

In the first place the composer is aware of words. Two-thirds
of the task of composing an opera consists of setting words to
music. The composer starts with a set of words – based on a
legend, a play, a novel, or else specially written for his purpose –
which is called a *libretto*. He decides which passages shall be
given to which voices and then sets them in song-form. The
nature of the song-form depends on many considerations, which
we shall discuss. The other one-third of the task lies in the composition of instrumental music. Some of this is also directly
inspired by words; as in the case of descriptive music – like that,
for example, in the 'Royal Hunt and Storm' in Berlioz's *The
Trojans*, or in the 'Sea Interludes' in Britten's *Peter Grimes*.
(These pieces are heard separately from the operas as concert-
pieces, and are also available in excellent recordings.) We must,
however, remember that at a certain point words diminish in
importance, so that music alone carries the opera forward. A
successful opera-composer must be sensitive to words. He must
find out how to give them proper accentuation. He must decide
if a word needs one musical note or many, and whether and
how these notes lie in relation to one another. He must feel the
colour of a word and reflect this colour in his music.

One of the great masters of English song was Henry Purcell
(1659–95). He was also a great dramatic composer. We may see
how he tackled the problem of dealing with words so as to give
the maximum of dramatic effect in the most economical way.
The orchestral prelude (very short, and only for strings and
harpsichord) to Act V of *King Arthur* describes a storm. Aeolus,
the God of the Winds, appears 'in a cloud above'. He orders the
unruly winds to stop misbehaving, and tells them to: (Ex. 1.)
The way in which that word is sung is only different from

Ex.1

Re-tire,   re - tire,   re-tire,   re - tire.

the way it is spoken because of the exactness of the pitch relationships. The accentuation is the same. We do notice that because
the whole passage descends over more than an octave the idea
contained in the words of going back – or away – is emphasised.
The notes go further and further away from their starting-point :
it is as simple as that. But how effective this simplicity of musical
statement is !

Purcell knows what is coming. He has taken his melody down
so that it can go up again. (Ex. 2.)

Ex.2

and let Bri - tan - nia rise, _____

Again the idea of the words is reinforced by the shaping of the
musical phrase. But still, so far as accentuation is concerned, we
are not very far from speech.

Purcell repeats the words 'retire, and let Britannia rise', and
uses more or less the same musical shape. Then he finishes the
sentence : (Ex. 3.) Here we are much further away from the

Ex.3

In tri - - - - - - umph o'er the main.

spoken language, for no one would require all that time in which
to say 'triumph'. But this is where we consider the colour of a
word, and the many aspects of one idea that live *behind* a word.
This word has a ring to it, and we may very well think of the
sound of the trumpet which sounds on a triumphant occasion.
Half-way through the phrase Purcell gives us the kind of pattern
we associate with the trumpet. He gives many notes to the one
word because the mastery required by the singer is also sugges-
tive : of the mastery and power which adds up to a triumph.

This triumph is 'O'er the main'; that is, the sea. That the sea is a wide stretch of water, Purcell suggests by his last three notes.

There is more to it than this. Purcell is being patriotic, and is really emphasising the hope of the Englishmen of his day that Britannia with her ships would command the waves!

In these examples from one small section of an opera the accompaniment to the voice is not very important. The further back we go in point of time so far as opera is concerned the more important is the voice and the less important the accompaniment.

Purcell lived in the second half of the seventeenth century. It was only at the beginning of that century that the art of opera began to show itself in a form that we should now recognise as operatic in any modern sense.

The men who were responsible for the earliest operas of our tradition were Italian.

There was a nobleman, the Count of Vernio, Giovanni Bardi; there was his aristocratic friend Jacopo Corsi; there was Ottavio Rinuccini, a poet; and there were two professional musicians, Giulio Caccini (about 1545–1618) and Jacopo Peri (1561–1633). They all met in Florence.

During the period of the Renaissance – a period in which men sought new ideas in every direction – the cities of Italy, each a separate State, were the chief centres of cultural development. The aristocracy supported artists, and writers, and musicians. Not only did rich men put aside money for the arts, but they frequently took an active part. This was more important than merely supplying money. They founded more or less informal societies (which later on became more formal) for the discussion of ideas. Many of these societies centred on literature. It was difficult in Italy, however, to talk about poetry without also talking about music, because the two arts were so closely bound together. For Giovanni Bardi poetry and music were the all-important topics.

Habits do not change very much. When a group gets together for discussion it is not long before someone begins to criticise. Very often what appears to be 'old-fashioned' is hardest hit. For most men of spirit wish to go forward.

When Bardi assembled his friends together the most popular way of setting words to music was in the manner of the madrigal. In a madrigal, which is laid out for singing in three, four, five, or more parts, the detail of words gets lost. Bardi considered that if words were sung they should be clearly heard. The poet Rinuccini, as might be expected, agreed with him.

Bardi was interested in drama, for dramatic performances were part and parcel of the aristocrat's way of life. There was hardly a festival occasion which was not celebrated with some kind of specially composed play or pageant. These, too, needed music. He was also interested in the literature and drama of classical Greece. Men of that age were, for they looked back to that classical period as to a golden age. The culture of Greece had a very great influence on Renaissance man.

In Greek drama, it was thought, words were declaimed to the accompaniment of the lyre. This, said Bardi, should be the foundation of reformed song. The words of such fine poets as the greatest of the Italian masters – Dante – and the most notable living poet, Rinuccini, would then make sense when sung.

Vincenzo Galilei, son of the famous astronomer, was the first to put the new ideas into practice. He set to music a passage from Dante's *Divine Comedy*, in which the voice part was more dramatic than was the case in the madrigals of the day, and in which it was clear that the words were of first importance. The kind of vocal music in which emphasis was placed on the words and in which the accentuation of the words controlled that of the melodic line, was called *recitative*. The development of recitative was vital to the tradition of dramatic music.

It is elsewhere emphasised that composers are best able to put their ideas into shape when they are thoroughly practical in approach. Jacopo Peri was a skilled singer and popular with those who listened to music in the palaces of Florence. He was conscious, it might seem, of the need for displaying a 'personality' – rather in the modern sense. He had golden hair, and he wore it long. That was why he was generally known by the nickname of 'Il Zazzerino' ('The long-haired'). He was used to arranging music for all kinds of social occasions, and in 1597 it was suggested to him by Jacopo Corsi and Rinuccini that a dramatic work based on the latest theories of speech-rhythm music should be devised.

The subject chosen was that of Apollo and Daphne. Daphne, a daughter of the river Peneus, was loved by Apollo, or Phoebus, the sun-god. Wishing to escape from Apollo Daphne asked the gods to help her. They did. They changed her into a laurel. The laurel became the favourite tree of Apollo! This may not be everybody's idea of a story, but it appealed to those who, like the Florentine intellectuals, thought that everything that was classical was right.

When *Dafne* was performed at the house of Corsi it caused a great stir. This, considered to be the first opera, was produced on a number of occasions. We may note that *Dafne* was a team effort. Rinuccini provided the words, and Peri most of the music; but some of the words were also set by Corsi. Peri sang in the opera, and Corsi played the harpsichord. Unfortunately the greater part of the music was subsequently lost, though some part of Corsi's settings survive in a manuscript preserved in Brussels.

In 1600 Henry IV, King of France, was to marry Maria di Medici, a member of the most important family in Florence – indeed in Italy – during the period of the Renaissance and for long afterwards. In order to celebrate the occasion worthily – and also to impress the distinguished members of the French Court who were present in Florence – it was decided to commission Peri to compose another work similar to *Dafne*. The result of this proposal was *Euridice*. Euridice was the wife of Orpheus – the god of music – who died from a snake-bite, went to the

'infernal regions' where Orpheus followed her in the hope of
bringing her back. . . . A promising story!

The music for this, highly successful entertainment, has survived, and we can see how Peri put the idea of opera into
practical form.

The basis of *Euridice* was recitative. This was mostly accompanied by the harpsichordist (Jacopo Corsi) who played from a
bass line along which figures were set by the composer to indicate
which chords should be used. The player was thus free to
improvise within the limits set by the *figured bass*. Recitative
may *look* dry simply as notes on paper. In performance it should
never sound so. The singer is expected to give the full power of
the words in the most effective way possible. Within this context
the most effective will also be the most dramatic way. We know
that Peri was a good singer. We may be sure that he showed all
his expressive talent in what was his most important work to
date. We may see that a good deal was left to the performer,
whether instrumental or vocal, to decide at the time of rehearsal
and even performance. The element of extemporisation remained
important for a long time to come. Here are the bare bones of a
passage of Peri; recitative. Orpheus, in Hell, must make this
sound suitably gloomy. (Ex. 4.)

Ex. 4

Fu-ne-ste piag-ge   om-bro-si or-ri-do   cam-pi   che di stel-le, o di

so-le   Non ve-de-ste gi à | mai scin-til-l'ò lam-pi

*(O evil shores, dismal,
horrific plains; the
light of stars and of
sun is never to be
seen.)*

Euridice, however, was not *all* recitative. Peri, as every other composer of dramatic music knows, knew that the success of a dramatic performance depended on contrast. Therefore this opera contained some brief choruses – but simpler in style than madrigals. The final chorus was also extended into a dance, thus linking the work with ballet – also an important and popular courtly entertainment of those days.

The instruments used were few : harpsichord, two lutes, a lyre, and a 'triple' flute. The latter instrument has an important passage, played on stage by a shepherd named Thyrsis. The flute who reminded the more imaginative members of the orchestra of the flute players they may have seen on ancient pottery, or about whom they had certainly read. Also the sound of the flute was associated with the open-air, and the countryside. The orchestra in a modern sense did not then exist. But the principle of using the tone-colours of instruments – which is the foundation of orchestral techniques – was well understood. Most of all in dramatic music, where associations of particular sounds with particular ideas persisted from earlier dramatic traditions.

When first performed, *Euridice* was esteemed because it had as much appeal to an audience as any modern work that we find attractive has for us. If we heard a performance today, however, we should find it difficult to be moved in the same way, unless we could put out of mind all later ideas as to what opera is.

Peri had started more than he knew. Nevertheless he realised that he was on the verge of something significant, and when *Euridice* was published he included a Preface in which he set out his ideas in some detail. In this Preface he said that in all his compositions he had always tried to concentrate on 'imitating' by way of music the feeling – or sentiment – expressed by the words; and that he had endeavoured to use notes in the manner proper to all good singing.

Where did Giulio Caccini stand in all this? He too was a fine

singer (so was his daughter, who is said to have taken the part of
Euridice in Peri's work) and an equally fine composer: a better
composer in fact than Peri. Indeed he was not altogether pleased
at Peri's success, particularly since he had contributed some
numbers to Peri's *Euridice*. In due course Caccini re-set both
Dafne and *Euridice*, but his greatest achievement lay in his
expressive settings of poems that were, however, independent of
music-drama.

In 1602 Caccini published one of the landmarks in the
development of vocal music. Appropriately enough this was
called *Le nuove musiche* (*The New Music*). This collection of
solo songs and madrigals – which may still be heard with
pleasure – demonstrated many different possibilities. Caccini
showed varied ways of setting words expressively – by the use of
particular intervals, by the ornamentation of passages, by the
repetition of 'verses' and so on. He was not only one of the
founders of opera, but also of modern solo song.

In the intellectual atmosphere in which he moved it was
hardly surprising that Caccini also should issue a declaration of
his principles in a Preface. The Preface to *The New Music* has
been, as it were, a kind of bible to later composers of opera
anxious to re-assert the basic ideas. '. . . I had', he said, 'the idea
of introducing a form of music which would make it posssible
to speak in music. In order to compose and to sing effectively in
this style, it is necessary to have a proper appreciation of the
"idea" and the words. . . .' He went on to say that as he saw it
vocal music in the first place should 'be speech and rhythm, and
[musical] sound only in the second place – not the other way
round'. This part of his message was seized on, and acted on,
by later notable reformers of opera, especially Gluck and
Wagner.

By this time almost everything that it is necessary to know
about the principles on which drama can be associated with
music had been stated. These principles were first tried out before

a select audience. The first *music-drama*, as it was called, was a special kind of entertainment for a special kind of people (as they thought themselves). Something of the aristocratic sense still lingers; most obviously when Heads of States take other Heads of States (whether they like it or not) to an opera house. On these occasions the music critic is subordinate to the gossip writer and the fashion expert. Attention is paid to the audience rather than to the performers!

Nevertheless opera is now no longer narrowly aristocratic. In some countries, indeed, it is genuinely popular and the star singer is as much sought after for autographs as the star sportsman – or sportswoman.

To this day the most popular operas, and also some of the greatest, are Italian. So too are many of the famous singers. Of those who are not Italian-born the majority have proved themselves by their mastery of the Italian style. Since Italy was the home of opera this was not surprising.

It is, however, a far cry from a small group of pioneers in the Florence of time past, to, say, the amateur opera team in some provincial town in Britain or America wrestling with a performance of Puccini's *Madame Butterfly*. The line along which we travel from the one point to the other is the line of song, and of singing technique. The Italians made song a medium for the clear expression of feelings.

Bardi and his colleagues started out with this intention. First of all they stripped down the engine of music, and having partly re-assembled it, left it to others to carry on from where they left off. If you listen to one of the earliest operas you may feel that there is something missing. What you will probably find not there is what is most easily, if not quite accurately, described as 'tunefulness'. But tunefulness soon came in, in a big way.

A music drama depended on collaboration. The composer was one member of a team. We may think him the most important

member of the team (though the prestige of the designer of
the sets and also of the producer is considerable today), but it
was not always so. Rinuccini, the poet, thought that his work
in making a libretto was the most important. It was not long
before singers made it quite clear that they were the real
making of an opera. Since an opera can get nowhere without
the whole-hearted support of singers it is hardly surprising
that at an early stage the wishes of singers had a great deal of
influence.

The seventeenth century was a great age of singers. It was the
age in which the professional singer emerged as a personality in
his or her own right. The opera was an important factor in
ensuring this, for what an audience expected of a singer was
brilliance on the one hand and a wealth of expression on the
other. The singer was encouraged in both directions by the
development of opera.

The most gifted of the early school of Italian opera-composers
was Claudio Monteverdi (1567–1643). Monteverdi composed
many operas (of which a considerable number were lost) between
1607 (*Orfeo*) and 1642 (*L'Incoronazione di Poppea*). He built
outwards from the basic principles. Thus his voice parts were
more varied than previously and his instrumental accompaniments essential to the full expression of the plot. Monteverdi
understood that recitative was invaluable but that an extended
type of word-setting in which the melodic line carried ideas that
belonged to music more than to words also had a part to play.
By exploring different ways of using the solo voice he naturally
endeared himself to singers. Similarly, by exploiting instrumental
devices that had not previously been sanctioned in public performances he won the regard of players. Both ways Monteverdi
gained the approval of audiences.

Recitative stands on one side of vocal music. On the other is
what is called *aria*. Recitative looks towards the words : aria looks
away from and beyond them. By the middle of the seventeenth

century the pattern of aria was stylised. The flowing quality of the Italian aria called for concentrated effort on the part of singers. They aimed to perfect their tone. So important was this matter of tone that the style of singing then cultivated what was called *bel canto* (*'beautiful singing'*). A singer spent many years perfecting his art. As always good teachers were rare, but less rare in Italy than elsewhere.

Opera was started in a small way. It was not long after the Florentines had launched their project that many palaces in Italy boasted a theatre. Opera spread to European courts and after the Restoration of the Monarchy in England in 1660 there was a good deal of initiative displayed in London in operatic production. Meanwhile something of great significance had happened in Venice. In 1637 the first public opera-house, that named San Cassiano, was opened in the city, and because fine singers were hired proved immensely popular.

Before the end of the seventeenth century there were sixteen theatres in Venice, all vying with each other in the production of operas. Since there were 358 new operas produced in that one city within a period of sixty-three years it can be seen how popular opera became. A Venetian style was established, and certain composers transplanted it in other countries. Pietro Cavalli was called to Paris in 1660 to direct his *Sense* (*Xerxes*) as part of the festivities held in celebration of the marriage of King Louis XIV. Antonio Caldara, a Venetian, worked in Rome and Madrid before settling down as deputy musical director at the Court of Vienna. He composed more than one hundred operas. Heinrich Schütz, one of the greatest of German composers, studied in Venice, and when he went home advocated the virtues of Italian opera. Since the marriage of the daughter of the Count of Hesse in 1627 afforded a golden opportunity he composed an opera for the occasion.

If you had been in Italy in those days you made sure that everybody was aware of it. If you could compose in the Italian style so much the better. Schütz took Rinuccini's libretto of *Dafne*, had it translated into German and then set it to music. Alas! the music has not survived. This is not surprising, for much was destroyed in Germany during the Thirty Years War that was waged from 1618 to 1648.

Italy in the seventeenth century was not a unified country, with one central government. It comprised many separate states, each with its own constitution and government. Between the great cities there was intense rivalry. This helped in the development of opera because no court, or city, was content to appear backward in comparison with another.

One of the most active musical centres in Italy was Naples, then part of the Spanish dominions. Alessandro Scarlatti (1660–1725) worked in Naples for different periods in a busy and distinguished life – he held posts also in Florence and Rome – and he contributed greatly to the Neapolitan opera tradition. He composed more than one hundred operas in which were wonderful arias that enchanted singers and audiences alike. The pattern which Scarlatti established – of an opening section, a contrasted middle section, and a varied repeat of the first section – held fast for a long time to come. The *da capo* aria as it was known (*da capo* meaning 'from the beginning') is to be found in the vocal works of Henry Purcell and also of his brother Daniel, Bach, Handel, Telemann, Hasse, Arne, and many other composers of the Baroque era.

Scarlatti perfected one form of opera overture – known as the 'Italian' overture since Lully in Paris evolved a different form of overture described as the 'French' overture. He showed how many kinds of emotion could be pictured in arias – some were 'pastoral', some were 'martial', some were 'pathetic', some were 'brilliant', and so on – and he also realised exactly what the powers of the human voice were.

A great idea comes to fruition at a time when many favourable conditions are to hand. Scarlatti benefited from the availability of fine singers, from the work that many others had put into the shaping of opera, and from the fact that during his lifetime the arts of making and playing the violin – and members of the violin family – were perfected. He was also fortunate in that all the branches of music acted upon one another. Oratorio (which is dealt with in some detail in the next chapter) and opera·were close companions, while in between there was the cantata – a sequence of recitatives and arias often heard on a text that was of a dramatic character – which was a regular feature of private music-meetings.

Before long many great theatres were built. Leopold I, himself a composer, instituted an opera-house in Vienna as early as 1659. The first opera-house in Hamburg – where Handel played the violin as a young man – was opened in 1678. The beautiful theatre of San Carlo, built at enormous expense by Charles III, was opened in Naples in 1737. A theatre had been erected in Milan in 1717. A little more than half-a-century later it was, like many other buildings in those days, destroyed by fire. Heartbroken, the opera-promoters of Milan looked for a new site. They discovered one near the ancient church of St Maria alla Scala. The new theatre was known as 'La Scala'. The architect was Giuseppe Piermarini (1734–1808). This, perhaps, was to become the most famous opera-house in the world.

Throughout the eighteenth century the Italian style of opera was almost universal, and Italian composers, directors and singers dominated opera-houses all over Europe. There were two main kinds of opera. On the one hand there was *opera seria*, the subjects of which were always 'heroic'; on the other there was *opera buffa*, or comic opera, discussed in Chapter 11.

Italian musicians had brought music within the theatre to a high peak of efficiency in all departments. In so doing they had provided a plan which any trained librettist and composer could follow. The composer knew he must provide an overture, so many

recitatives and arias (suitably varied according to well understood conventions), duets, and ensemble numbers. It was
moderately easy to write a passable *opera seria*. Many lesser
composers gave way to the growing demands of the singers – who
earned fabulous incomes – and were content to provide material
of which the principle purpose was to show off the voice. The
orchestra became relegated to a subordinate position. In case it
should be thought that everybody thought that everything was
marvellous it is worth mentioning that there were those who
went to the opera merely because it was the done thing but who
were bored with what went on.

About 1740 Cardinal de Tencin, exaggerating somewhat,
remarked to a French visitor in Rome that it was tedious to have
to sit through five hours (the performances were considerably
lengthened by the intervals) of almost uninterrupted recitative, in
order to hear two or three decent airs. Another clergyman, the
Abbé Franquini, met a lady who seemed to be enjoying a stretch
of recitative. 'Madam,' he said, 'I see you like listening to
sermons.'

Among the more serious minded it was clear that something
had gone wrong with opera.

In addition to this there was an increasing reluctance to accept
the primacy of Italian music as a matter of principle. France
had taken opera in one direction. Germany, where the play with
music known as the *Singspiel*, had drawn it in another. In
England where audiences thought more of plot and action than
of music and where many influential men spoke out against the
tyranny of the Italian language the ballad opera (see page 177f.)
formed an independent tradition.

But opera in Italy had become part of the life of the country,
and truly popular art – as it is today. It remained the great
training ground of Italian musicians, and across the centuries
artists from other lands continued to visit the Italian opera-
houses to study the basic techniques of opera performance. Above

all, Italy was the land of song. *Bel canto* stood firm as an ideal. As we listen to the music of Bellini, Donizetti, Rossini, Verdi, Mascagni, and Puccini, we understand how firm this ideal has stood the test of time.

IX

Sacred Opera, or Oratorio

THE period of the Renaissance was one in which men asked many questions. Sometimes they found answers, and when they did it was felt that progress had been made. Sometimes the questions were too difficult for answers to be found. Indeed some of these questions are still with us.

When you come to think of it certain questions can never be answered. The two main fields in which unanswerable questions lie are politics and religion. In searching for answers, however, men sometimes hit on ideas which in themselves are of benefit and value. We should also remember that different men have different ways of tackling great problems. The men whom at first we find most interesting are those who are described as 'men of action'.

It is worth mentioning here that musicians should truthfully be thought of as belonging to the class of 'men of action'. In general they are not thought of in this way; but their work is so much connected with *doing* and *making* that it is impossible to consider them as not at least being extremely active.

The musician, however, is often to be found working with, or for, another man – or group of men – whose careers are more obviously active in a more accepted sense. Curiously, the music that is, or should be, most active in itself is religious music in its many forms. The composer of this kind of music may not believe that he is going to change the world by his music (though some may do), but his employer certainly believes that he ought to. The great religious leaders have all made quite deliberate use of music with the intention of affecting the way in which people feel and think.

Many religious leaders have been grateful to musicians who sometimes, independently, may seem to have done their work for them. In 1966 the American magazine *Time* reported that a group of Roman Catholic priests had tried to suggest that Johann Sebastian Bach should be given the title of 'Blessed'. Their knowledge not being equal to their zeal they were unaware that Bach belonged to the Protestant, Lutheran, Church in his lifetime. However, the thought was a worthy one, for Bach's great works for the church – his *St John* and *St Matthew Passions*, *Mass in B Minor*, church cantatas and *Christmas Oratorio* – cross all kinds of frontiers, and enable thousands in different lands to value their convictions the more.

The same is true of Handel's *Messiah* which across more than two hundred years has moved countless people, of all faiths, or, indeed, of none. The four most famous bars are quoted at the head of the chapter. *Messiah* is called an oratorio. Why is it called an oratorio?

As we have seen, particular kinds of music come into existence often in order to meet some need, or in response to some activity, that belong to a wider field than that of music. Opera, as we know it, was one result of Renaissance thought. Oratorio was another. In fact oratorio, in a modern sense, got off the ground at the same time as opera.

In early times it was rarely possible to draw a line between religious and secular art. This was especially true of drama. In the fifteenth and early sixteenth centuries the Miracle or Mystery Plays, based on Bible stories or on lives of the Saints, were religious in their subject matter. But in treatment they were often anything but religious. The shepherds of the Nativity plays – to take one instance – were frequently treated as figures of comedy.

The Reformation, however, tended to separate the 'sacred' from the 'secular', and this separation has proved disastrous in many ways, if only because what is 'sacred' has often been treated in a dull manner. A Roman priest of the sixteenth century saw this danger, and tried to prevent it. To him we are indebted for the *idea* of oratorio.

In the sixteenth as in the twentieth century there were many ministers of religion who were trying to bring an old faith up-to-date, in order to make it acceptable. The Roman Catholic Church was aware of a need for change, and during that century set up a great Council of the Church to determine what could be done. A great man does not wait until the findings of a council have been translated into normal activity. He moves ahead, independently.

Philip Neri was one of the most conspicuous figures in Rome in the mid-sixteenth century. He was known to be a good man, to have a particular interest in young people, and to have unusual and unconventional ideas. He loved talking, but because he knew when to stop and was also a good listener he encouraged conversation : the sharing of ideas. He allowed his friends and followers to discuss anything they wished to bring up. In this way he gathered round him a large and varied group of men and women. On the whole, and compared with the 'academies' of Florence this group was less narrowly aristocratic.

Philip Neri used the Church of St Mary as his headquarters, but in summer weather he took his disciples for walks into the country in order to enjoy both mental and physical stimulation. The group which was led by Philip Neri prayed together. Their church came to be known as an Oratory – which means a place in which to pray. The group therefore was known as 'the Oratorians'. We already see the shape of the word with which we started.

Among the friends of Neri were many musicians. As we have seen the end of the sixteenth century was a lively period in the history of music. Since music played an important part in life it was freely and generally discussed.

What shall we do about church music? This was a burning question that was being asked when Neri was busy in Rome. It was a burning question because many thought that the masses and motets that were sung were too complicated. When music for voices was complicated it became impossible to hear the words. And the words were more important than the music to which they were set in the eyes of the leaders of the church.

But the importance of words in relation to music was also being emphasised elsewhere. It was from examining this matter that the idea of opera, or 'drama through music' developed.

One of the close friends of Philip Neri was Giovanni Animuccia, Director of Music at the Vatican from 1555 until his death in 1571. Neri admired Animuccia as man and musician. As he often used colourful language he declared after his friend's death that he had seen Animuccia's soul fly up to heaven!

During his lifetime Animuccia composed music for the Oratory. His famous songs, which were performed after the regular services had taken place, were settings of verses by a late

medieval Italian poet known as Jacopone di Todi. Animuccia's
songs, inspired by the theories otherwise being worked out by
Peri and Caccini in Florence, were more dramatic in character
than the general run of church songs.

In the Oratory musicians were given opportunity to experiment. So it was that in 1600 another composer was able here to
produce an experimental work. This was Emilio de' Cavalieri,
a native of Rome who had, however, worked in Florence.
There he had become friendly with Giovanni Bardi and those
around him of whom we have already read in the previous
chapter.

By this time Philip Neri was dead. But his influence was still
powerful. He was regarded as a Saint and there were many
legends about him. It was indeed said that on one occasion he
had visited the palace of the Massimo family in Rome, where
one of the sons of the house lay dead and that he had restored
the boy to life. Since this was unlikely to have happened we may
prefer to think that what St Philip did for music was a more
credible miracle.

The work which Emilio de' Cavalieri produced in the Oratory
in February 1600, was called 'The Representation of the Soul
and the Body'. It was an allegory, in which Time, the World,
Pleasure, the Soul, and the Body – and so on, were made to
appear as persons. The intention of the writer of an allegory was
to teach a lesson. This was in keeping with the views of the
Fathers of the Church at that time. It was also in keeping with
the general attitude of church leaders at all times.

The Representation was very little different from a music
drama of the same period except for the more intentionally
instructive nature of the subject. The work consists for the most
part of recitative, accompanied by a 'figured bass' – the operation
of which Cavalieri explained in his Preface. There are some
choruses – of good spirits and bad spirits, which were made more
expressive by the composer's use of an 'echo' device. The instru-

mentation was simple; harpsichord, lutes, lyre, organ (possibly optional) and flutes. The performers were suitably dressed for their parts, and there was scenery – behind which the instrumentalists were hidden.

In one respect *The Representation* was ahead of opera. It was divided into three sections, called acts, between which interludes could be played. Cavalieri, who said that he meant his work to be listened to by all kinds of people, was by no means insistent that the work should be performed only in church. It was, he said, quite possible in a theatre or a hall, where up to one thousand spectators could be accommodated. It was by chance rather than by design that *The Representation* was first performed in a church. And it happened that the church was an Oratory. It was natural to invent a word to describe this kind of work. The word was *oratorio*.

Much credit for the broadening of the character of church music goes to St Philip Neri. But he was not alone in promoting new and vital ideas. Among the notable figures of the sixteenth century were also St Ignatius Loyola, founder of the Society of Jesus, and St Francis Xavier, a member of the Society of Jesus, famous as a missionary in the Far East. Like St Philip, although their views on organisation were different, these men were determined to take their message to the common people. They were also greatly respected during their lives and their memories revered when they were dead. Philip Neri, Ignatius Loyola, and Francis Xavier, were canonised – that is, given the title of Saint – on the same day – May 22, 1622.

As we have noticed St Philip drew to him many musicians. The Jesuits on the other hand proved a greater inspiration to painters. Among the painters who had Jesuit sympathies were Michelangelo (Merisi) Caravaggio and Gianlorenzo Bernini. The mark of a new style in painting in Italy at this time was a more free treatment of subjects; sometimes more colourful, sometimes more realistic, sometimes both. The intention of painters such as

Caravaggio, the Carracci family, the later Bernini, and their followers, was to make painting more expressive. Their aim was similar to that of the forward-looking musicians.

Both opera and oratorio had a strong association with the visual arts from the start. In respect of opera this association remained strong, in the case of oratorio it quickly weakened. However, at the critical period at the beginning of the seventeenth century there was encouragement to those who wished to join the arts together within the Church.

In one of the Decrees of the Council of Trent (which ended in 1563) it was stated that 'by means of the stories of the mysteries of our Redemption portrayed by paintings or other representations, the people [should] be instructed and confirmed in the habit of remembering, and continually turning over in their minds, the articles of the faith'. Thus, it was probably quite a deliberate act on Cavalieri's part to choose the title *Representation*. The stress laid by the Fathers of the Council on the value of the arts as a medium of teaching was, of course, a throw-back to the practice of the Middle Ages.

After Cavalieri's pioneer work there was something of a lull. Composers were still hard at work writing masses and motets for which there was a steady market, while the drama-conscious composers of Florence had no great incentive to turn aside from their preoccupations with secular music-drama.

The canonisation of three greatly loved saints, however, suggested how the forms of music-drama could be used in church. In 1622 an oratorio type of work in honour of St Ignatius and St Francis was performed with great success in one of the colleges in Rome. The composer was not an Italian, but a German (of noble birth) working in Rome. His name was Johann Kapsberger, also known as a composer of operas. Another work in honour of St Ignatius was composed in 1622 by Vittorio Loreto, a famous singer. These performances owed as much to the quality of singing, of the dresses, and of the decorations, as to that of the music. And they set a fashion which many were to follow during the next twenty or thirty years.

Just as the painters illustrated the lives of saints, or biblical episodes, so did the musicians take the same subjects to illustrate in terms of music. The painters used the same skills and techniques whether they were treating secular or sacred subjects. The former, as in opera, was often taken from classical mythology. Composers were a little less ready to do this. This was partly because, whereas opera was strong in Florence, Naples and in Venice, oratorio first established itself in Rome. But it was partly due to the power of the age-old tradition of church music. Opera composers did not introduce choral music except sparingly. Composers of church music were always aware of the presence of the church choir, and ready to make use of it.

Choral music became entrenched in early oratorio and there are fine movements in the works of Giovanni Carissimi, whose *Jephtha* is still performed. But Carissimi knew well how to handle solo voices and in *Jephtha* his power of vivid expression can be readily appreciated in the solo and duet sections.

One of the outstanding composers within the Italian oratorio tradition is Alessandro Scarlatti, who was a pupil of Carissimi, and whose importance in the field of opera has already been discussed (see pages 134–135). A master of almost every form of music of the age Scarlatti ranged widely over many fields of expression. This being the case there was, so far as technique was concerned, no division between opera and oratorio. Scarlatti composed oratorios over a period of some forty years, between 1680 and 1722. His works of this order numbered more than twenty and they were performed not only in Rome, but also in Modena, Florence, Naples, Venice and Vienna.

Although the musical structure of the oratorio of the late seventeenth century was more or less indistinguishable from that of opera, except for the greater importance of the chorus in more ambitious works, action and scenery were gradually discontinued.

This began effectively to divide the one type of music drama from the other.

The reason for this discontinuation was the one you would expect. After the initial period of relative freedom within the Church a reactionary mood settled on many of its leaders. A church, they urged, should not be mistaken for a theatre.

We now arrive at a paradox. The oratorios that we know best were composed with the intention of performance within the theatre. But the full resources of the theatre were not allowed to be used. By the end of Handel's life his oratorios were finding their way back to the church!

The general idea of oratorio originated with St Philip Neri. *Our* idea of oratorio originated with Handel. Was there any connection between the two ideas? As you might reasonably suspect, there was.

Handel, already a fine composer, went to Italy at the age of twenty-one. He remained in Italy for nearly four years. While he was there he met the principal Italian composers and so mastered the Italian style of composition that he enjoyed a very high reputation indeed. Naturally the works that he wrote were consciously shaped with the taste of Italian audiences and performers in mind. The cantatas, operas, and oratorios, composed by Handel at this time show considerable familiarity with the music of Alessandro Scarlatti, as well as of other notable composers.

Handel composed one oratorio, *La resurrezione (The Resurrection)*, which was performed in a palace in Rome immediately after one had been given by Scarlatti. It should be noted that oratorios were in favour in Rome because operas were temporarily out of favour. When *La resurrezione* was first performed the Pope was not pleased that Handel had employed a woman singer to take part. A little later Handel composed an oratorio at the request of one of the famous 'academies' of Rome. This, like the first oratorio of Cavalieri, was allegorical and entitled

Il trionfo del tempo e del disingano. This means *The Triumph of Time and Truth* and it was under that title that a revised version of the oratorio was given in London almost fifty years later.

For the moment we may leave the Italian oratorio of the early eighteenth century and look towards England – where Handel was to make his home. Although Italian style was carefully studied by English composers it was not quite such a powerful influence as it might have been. This was because of the strength of the tradition of the music of the Church of England. At its best this was responsible for a large number of masterly works, in the form of settings of biblical texts. These works were anthems. The English anthem of the early eighteenth century was frequently designed on a large scale, for great events, State occasions, and royal celebrations all called for suitable music. An anthem by Henry Purcell, or William Blow, or William Croft, contained recitatives, arias, and sometimes duets. Above all it contained much chorus music. The anthem for the great occasion was accompanied by orchestra, which often had an independent movement – a 'symphony' as it was called – to play. The form used for the English anthem also served for extended settings of the *Te Deum* (with the English words of the Prayer Book).

Handel had not been long in England before he was required to compose a setting of the *Te Deum* to be sung in St Paul's Cathedral in order to celebrate the ending of the War of Spanish Succession by the signing of the Peace Treaty of Utrecht. The *Utrecht Te Deum*, in which Handel blended something of the choral technique of English music with those methods he had perfected in the Italian vein, was performed on July 7, 1713.

Handel, however, had come to England with the main aim of composing Italian operas. This he did, at first with great success and profit. But as the years passed Italian opera passed out of favour in London. Friends advised Handel to set English rather than Italian texts to music. Between 1716 and 1718 he

had opportunity to compose anthems for the wealthy Duke of
Chandos who maintained his own chapel at his great house at
Canons, near Edgware. In 1719 Handel collaborated with the
poet John Gay (the author of *The Beggar's Opera* – see page 177)
and composed a beautiful Serenata, *Acis and Galatea*. A year
later, encouraged by a group of writers which included Alexander
Pope, he composed a work of similar design but on a biblical
subject. This was called *Haman and Mordecai*. The libretto of
this work told the story of Esther, the adopted daughter of
Mordecai. It was based not directly on the Book of Esther in
the Old Testament but on a drama on the subject by the French
writer Jean Racine. The story, although taken from a biblical
source, is not recognisably 'religious', but full of plot, incident,
and high drama. For his performances at Canons Handel used
singers whom he knew well, from the Chapel Royal and St
Paul's Cathedral.

In 1732 one of these singers, Bernard Gates, was the Master
(Music Director) of the Chapel Royal. A friend and admirer of
Handel he thought it sad that such a fine work as *Haman and
Mordecai* should be forgotten. He arranged a revival of it. This
revival came at an opportune moment. The feeling that English
works should take precedence over Italian operas was now very
strong. On May 2, 1732, *Haman and Mordecai*, now styled an
oratorio and re-titled *Esther*, was performed at the King's
Theatre, in the Haymarket, London.

The choristers of the Chapel Royal took part in this revival,
but a condition of the performance was that there should be no
acting on the stage. The oratorio was as dramatic as any opera,
and more dramatic than many of that period. It was divided into
acts as an opera. In the word-book which members of the
audience could buy one could read stage-direction, to show
what would have been happening on the stage if only acting had
been allowed.

The idea of oratorio caught on in London. The pattern both

of composition and performance set by *Esther* remained constant. During the next twenty years Handel wrote many oratorios. Mostly they were given in Covent Garden Theatre. Handel directed the performances, for which he engaged some Italian opera singers, a number of talented British singers, the faithful choristers of the Chapel Royal, and the best instrumentalists to be found in London. Between the acts he played the organ concertos which he composed for this purpose. These had considerable drawing power, for Handel was a fine organist.

For the most part the oratorios were based on Old Testament stories, always of a dramatic character. Among the best known are *Saul, Israel in Egypt* (in which the soloists have little to do and the chorus a great deal), *Samson,* and *Jephtha.* One oratorio, *Theodora,* is based on a Christian legend. There were works of similar structure right outside the biblical tradition, but which more than satisfied the English liking for this kind of entertainment. Among these were a setting of John Milton's *L'Allegro* which contains music that beautifully describes the English countryside, and one of William Congreve's *Semele.* Congreve had written this in 1708 in the form of an opera-book, hoping that it might start a tradition of English opera. Although it was set to music at that time by the Court composer John Eccles it did not make any impression. Handel's *Semele* is a fine work which is nowaday often given as an opera.

Whenever we think of oratorio we think of Handel. And when we think of Handel we think also of *Messiah,* for this is one of the most famous musical works ever written by anyone.

Messiah is not a 'story' in the sense that the other oratorios of Handel are. It is an account of the life and influence of Christ. In the second part of the work, the account of Christ's suffering, we are reminded that although Handel had been nationalised as British he was by birth German; for the music is expressive in a manner to be found in German settings of the *Passion,* of which there is an orchestral setting by Handel himself. *Messiah* was composed for the people of Dublin, in which city it was first performed on April 13, 1742. It was given its first performance to raise money for various charities. When it became well-known in England it served to support English charities also.

Handel was interested in one charitable foundation especially. This was the Foundling Hospital and in his later years he directed many performances of *Messiah* in the chapel of the Foundling Hospital.

During the latter part of Handel's life there was a strong moral influence at work among the English middle-classes. New religious impulses also came through the missionary zeal of John Wesley. *Messiah* fitted well into the prevailing social atmosphere and this explains why at one early stage it took precedence over the other oratorios. Handel was regarded therefore as a great composer of religious music and in England this aspect of his many activities has continued to be regarded as the most important.

As has been said the English love of choral music came by way of the large anthem with oratorio. The choruses of the oratorios of Handel were ready-made when in the latter part of the eighteenth century, and more particularly the beginning of the nineteenth century large amateur choral societies (often of working-class origin) were formed.

The oratorios of Handel were soon adopted in Germany, where many were quick to appreciate that the composer was a German although long resident in England. The first performance of *Messiah* in Hamburg took place in 1771, when it was conducted by the Englishman Michael Arne, son of the composer Thomas Augustine Arne.

In Vienna an Austrian diplomat, Gottfried van Swieten, who had been once accredited to the Prussian Government, came to love the great choral works of Handel and Bach and he engaged Mozart to fill out the orchestration of certain of Handel's works. One of these works was *Messiah*, and for a long time to come this was usually performed in Mozart's amplified form. Haydn heard Handel's oratorios in London and went home to Austria inspired to write works of this nature, which would, in any case, be very useful in Vienna. He composed *The Creation*, completed in 1798, and *The Seasons* (a non-religious work) first performed in 1801. Haydn became popular too; his oratorios together with those of Handel were the foundation of amateur music-making in America. We are reminded of this today, because the Handel and Haydn Society founded in Boston in 1815 is still flourishing.

The spread of choral music through the many societies founded in the nineteenth century encouraged many composers to produce oratorios. Too many, however, were but pale imitations of those of Handel. One which did stand out, and which continues in popularity, is Mendelssohn's *Elijah*, written for the Birmingham Festival of 1846. The first performance was conducted by the composer. Another great oratorio-type work connected with Birmingham, and first performed there in 1900, was Elgar's *The Dream of Gerontius*.

The poem, *The Dream of Gerontius*, which inspired Elgar, was written by Cardinal John Henry Newman, who had the greatest respect for the life and work of St Philip Neri. He founded an English body or oratorians in order to infuse English Catholic life with the ideals of the Roman saint. The original manuscript of Elgar's *Dream* was presented by the composer to the Oratory in Birmingham, where it remains. In Handel's oratorios the musical techniques were strongly influenced by Italian opera. Elgar was an admirer of Richard Wagner and in his oratorios – in addition to *The Dream* he wrote *The Apostles* and *The Kingdom* – there is much that was inspired by the musical techniques of Wagner's music-dramas.

Behind all music we find two strong pulls, one from the church, one from the theatre. Oratorios in the first place belonged to both traditions. In modern times the fact that oratorios stemmed from a theatre-in-a-church, as it were, has been once again set before us. We may now see Handelian oratorios performed as operas, sometimes in a theatre, sometimes in a church. Otherwise we may appreciate more modern works in oratorio form as those of Benjamin Britten (see page 111) which have been composed with a view to dramatic performance in church.

When you come to think of it we are back where we started, with St Philip Neri and his 'Oratorians'. Or perhaps we are further back still. When the mystery plays with music were performed they showed how the finest of religious thoughts could make use of secular forms. These plays were accepted as part of the way of life. In their hey-day men did not argue as to whether they were sacred or secular. That argument came later, and when it was at its height the players folded up and the plays disappeared. In drama and music secular and sacred might be separated from one another. Handel knew this. That is why he was a great composer of oratorios.

X

Ballet

"Zephyr"

Flutes

J. P. Rameau "Les Indes galantes"

etc.

L IKE everything else the arts are subject to variations of
fashion. Sometimes changes take place with bewildering
rapidity, as is the case with the most widely popular arts of
today. A record is at the top of the selling list one week, and a
month later at the bottom. A group of performers is acclaimed
throughout the land one year, and all but forgotten the next.
Art-forms of greater complexity change their relative position
rather more slowly. None the less changes take place. Art never
stands still.

Fifty years ago oratorio performances by massive choirs and

orchestras were a general entertainment. Today fewer people go to hear such performances. On the other hand productions of ballets – rare in the earlier years of this century – now have very wide appeal. That this is the case reflects certain considerable changes of attitude in society. That ballet is a great popular art of today is due in large measure to the long traditions of the great schools of ballet in Russia. The Kirov Ballet of Leningrad and the Bolshoi Ballet of Moscow are world-famous.

Ballet, like opera, is less an independent art than one produced from a combination of several arts. The basis of ballet is dancing. The word itself tells us this, for its root means to dance – thus we have the allied word 'ball'. Dancing, however, is not a self-sufficient art. It needs the accompaniment of music, more often of instrumental rather than vocal music.

Dances divide into two main groups. There are on the one hand dances in which we may take part. On the other there are dances designed for specially trained performers, whom we watch. Dances of the second kind frequently have a ritual meaning. Among them are many folk and allied dances which have or have had their place in religious ceremonial.

When dancing is a spectacle the dancers wear special costumes : even when it is a purely social activity it is not unknown for people to take great trouble over what they will wear, sometimes going so far as to wear 'disguises' or 'fancy dress'. The richer the dress the more striking the dance seems, for the more colourful the dress the further is it away from that of everyday life. Contrasts in dresses, which represent contrasts in character, and contrasts in dance steps and movements, and contrasts in accompanying music, represent a kind of narrative. A ballet, therefore, has a 'story', but, unlike opera, the story is not told through the medium of words.

When we are going to see a ballet we may read the story beforehand. In some ways this is a help. But we should not have to do any homework : what a ballet is about should be clear from what goes on on the stage. To be truthful a ballet is not meant to be 'explained'.

We must always understand that there are some ideas that words cannot express. These are the ideas that find expression in music, in dance, in sculpture, in painting.

Too often people use words as a prop when they should be willing to trust their own powers of imagination. Folk-dances of long ago were not explained beforehand : people however had no difficulty in *feeling* what their meaning was.

There is one aspect of ballet which is felt in this unconscious way; and this is the root of its present popularity. We are drawn to the ballet because it gives us an opportunity to enjoy the beauty and grace of the human form. This partly tells us why ballet is so widespread today, whereas fifty years ago it was not. In those days the puritan influence was still strong in many countries, and there were many restrictions on what might be performed in public. These restrictions were particularly strong in regard to the theatre.

When puritan ideas prevail religion and the theatre look upon each other as enemies : they should be allies.

The main pattern of ballet evolved naturally. In African tribal life the oldest forms of ballet are still practised. These are an essential part of the ceremonies that take place at the most important times of life. When young men come of age there are elaborate ceremonies. There are solemn, processional dances; there are grotesque dances, sometimes called masquerades. Each form of dance has its own type of music and accompanying instruments. Certain instruments are held as sacred, and may only be played by selected members of the tribe. Their instruments are thought to have special, even 'divine', powers.

Sometimes ritual dances are clearly narrative. Among the Ikere people of Nigeria a mythological *babalawo*, or medicine-man, named Sinsinguntinsin, was venerated. He had great power over hunters, and if any of these should disobey him he would make their forays into the bush fail. Once upon a time a body of huntsmen plotted to destroy the *babalawo*. The next day, the plot having been frustrated, the *babalawo* brought famine and drought to the village from which the hunters came.

In the end this miracle-worker disappeared for ever. He had, it was said, gone into a great rock that dominates the landscape. He was then called Olusunta, or *'He-who-lives-in-the-rock'*. Even at the present time the Olusunta rock is a place of pilgrimage, and each July an Olusunta festival takes place.

The story of the god-man Olusunta is told not through words but through mime and dancing. Such stories are really about the impulses and emotions that affect human behaviour. These impulses and emotions cannot be described by words. The language of movement, however, can be very expressive and full of meaning. If we stop to think about it we can discover how true this is from everyday experience. Our attitudes to people are marked to some extent by our, usually conscious, responses to the way in which they show personality through movement.

For a long time the Hungarian people were famous for their dancing, which was rooted in a belief in its expressive value. And ancient forms of dance were kept going spontaneously until well within living memory. One of the most celebrated dances was known as the *verbunkos*. This was performed when young men were recruited into the Austrian army. The *verbunkos* was a circle dance. In the middle of the circle of young men about to be called up – stood the recruiting officer. With each repetition of the melody fresh movements were improvised, so that an air-and-variations pattern was followed – but with the variations in the action of the dance rather than in the music itself.

Alongside the soldiers' dances were those of the shepherds. These took many forms, sometimes even developing into miniature pantomimes. In one dance belonging to the north of Hungary a swineherd would throw his hat to the ground, to represent a swine. A man acting as a thief would appear and try to take away the hat – or rather the swine of which it was the symbol. The swineherd, armed with an axe, tried to prevent him. All the while the music was played by the instruments made by the shepherds – bagpipes, pipes, zithers. Caught up in the action the spectators clapped their hands, stamped their feet or sang the tunes that the musicians played.

Soon the African dances will not be seen any more in their original setting, but ideas based on the long tribal tradition of mime and dancing are already inspiring individual artists, or groups of artists. In 1964 a 'dance drama' entitled *Creation*, in which ancient myths and dance and musical practices were brought together, was presented in the experimental theatre in the city of Ibadan.

The peasant dances of Hungary belong to yesterday rather than today, but they have proved the starting-point for the activities of the Hungarian State Company of Dance, Song and Music. This company first of all presented the national dances in their simple form. Next came the artistic preparation and performance of the longer and more narrative dance sequences. Finally larger works, some in three acts, were founded on subjects that belonged to the national ballad tradition. Throughout this period of development and expansion the dancers, having laboured long to reproduce the steps of the traditional dances, learned how to express emotions – love, anger, pain, birth, and so on – in a manner that would be understood by a modern audience.

One may go round the world collecting national dances. In almost every case there comes the point at which the environment of the dance changes. Quite briefly, the dance goes indoors, and becomes an activity of the theatre.

When the folk – or popular dance goes into their theatre it becomes an entertainment. But, depending on certain conditions, it may also retain something of its former significance. The element of ritual is not entirely lost. This may be learned from watching and listening to the greatest ballet of the twentieth century European tradition – Stravinsky's *The Rite of Spring*. Of the origin of this work Stravinsky once wrote : 'I saw in imagination a solemn pagan rite : sage elders, seated in a circle, watching a young girl dancing herself to death. They were sacrificing her to propitiate the god of Spring.'

In *The Rite of Spring*, even now striking in its rhythmic insistence, its powerful and vivid orchestration, in its overall effect, Stravinsky reminds us of our distant backgrounds. He tells us that primitive ideas still lie at the back of our minds; that primitive ideas (he quotes folk-song to make the point clear) are never to be forgotten by the artist; for what are called 'primitive' ideas are those which liberate us from false conceptions of art. This was also the meaning of the paintings of Paul Gauguin, who, as we have read, left the overcrowded artistic life of Paris and went to the South Seas in search of fresh and inspiring subjects and ideas.

In art there are two paths. One leads away from what is termed primitive. The other leads back to it. Which path is chosen depends to a large extent on the period in which the artist lives.

In the long period of time which covered the fulfilment of the ideas of the Renaissance those who lived in the chief cities and at the courts of Europe pushed what was thought to be primitive away – sometimes out of sight, sometimes out of mind. We look on the sixteenth and seventeenth centuries as a time of high achievement in the arts and the sciences. But there was then much cruelty and injustice; squalor and disease wrought fearful havoc. It was only a minority of the educated who felt unease about this, and only a minority of a minority who were prepared to do anything to improve matters. People who enjoyed privilege saw to it that they held on to what they possessed.

People of the lower ranks of society were treated as inferior. Often they were made objects of ridicule. In court entertain-

ments of the Renaissance period – in Italy, France, and England
– artisans, peasants, sailors and so on, were shown as comic
figures. On the other hand, since 'shepherds and shepherdesses'
had been idealised in classical literature and sculpture there was
a strong inclination to keep this tradition of make-believe.
Country life and its symbolic figures, of shepherds and shepherdesses, became remote from real life in another direction.
They seemed to live in a dream-world, too good to be true.

Ballet in what we may consider its 'natural' form, that is
within a folk tradition, is realistic – because the actions have a
direct connection with everyday life and thought. In such ballet
there is also a good deal that is fantastic, because, as has been
shown, everyday behaviour can appear as unusual and full of
comedy. The civilisation, or sophistication, of ballet took it in
the direction of fantasy and make-believe. The first home of
ballet, or the environment in which conditions helped it to
develop, was the Court of Louis XIV.

Louis XIV was known as 'Le roi soleil' – the 'sun king'. He
acquired this nickname from a ballet. The King was a keen
dancer and liked to take part in performances and in the year
1653 acted the mythological 'sun king' in the *Ballet of the Night*.
The title was applied to him by his courtiers and the king did
not object.

Louis XIV was one of the most powerful rulers of modern
Europe. Everything that could help to establish his reputation
assisted him to hold the rains of power more firmly. In an age in
which the arts were highly esteemed they had a considerable
political importance. A monarch who impressed foreign ambassa-
dors with his intellectual and artistic abilities and who could
show things not to be found anywhere else was half-way to being
an outstanding monarch. (Other qualities were necessary, of
course, as was shown in the case of Charles I of England, who
was well equipped on the artistic side but less fortunate on other
of his aptitudes.)

Ballet and opera came to Florence from Italy. So did the most famous composer of the French Court of the time of Louis XIV, Jean-Baptiste Lully (1632–87). Louis XIV was not only Lully's employer. His relationship with the musician was as close and generous as that of Prince Nicholas Esterházy with Haydn. The king also held the court dancing master Pierre Beauchamp, who was also a composer, in high esteem. The three men, together with poets, dramatists, painters, and technicians, worked closely together to revolutionise the art of dancing. When ballets were performed at the Court of Louis XIV the dancing was done by courtiers. There was a tradition of such participation in what was first thought of, and sometimes described as, an 'entertainment'. But there was another reason. The King liked to keep his noblemen under his supervision so that they could not get up to anything of which he disapproved. Practising ballet steps in fact kept them out of mischief!

Lully composed his first ballet for the French Court in 1653. He continued to compose music for this purpose until his death more than thirty years later. The dances which were the mainstay of the ballets of Lully were gavottes, minuets, chaconnes, bourrées, and gigues. In the course of time these dance forms became so widely popular that they invaded every kind of music, so that they are to be found in the keyboard and orchestral works of the great composers for many years. The most familiar of these dances, perhaps, is the minuet, which was carried over into the classical symphony.

Between them Louis XIV, Lully, and Beauchamp formalised the art of dancing. In 1662 a Royal Academy of Dancing was founded. Conventions hardened into rules, and all rules relating to dancing were issued from France. That is why to this day all the terms of ballet are French.

If we were able to retrace our steps in time and arrive at the Royal Palace in Paris on a day at the end of January in 1665 we should be able to see a ballet with music by Lully, with the

dances arranged by Beauchamp, and with the story – the mythological story – of *The Birth of Venus* written for the purpose of
this ballet by one of the Court poets, Isaac de Benserade. We
would be impressed by the fine playing of the orchestra, under
Lully's direction, the performance of the strings, especially, being
as fine as we would meet anywhere. We would be surprised that
the ballet, unlike any modern ones we know, included some
songs. The scenery would be magnificent. So too would be the
dresses.

But surely, we would think, these are not suitable dresses for
ballet. The men and women would merely be wearing their best
and most formal attire; very fine on State occasions, but decidedly
unwieldy for dancing. The King, however, insisted on formality
and magnificence in order to underline the sense of grandeur
that it was his aim to impart through the arts. As in earlier
times the dancers would only disguise themselves within the parts
they were supposed to represent by wearing masks.

Lully was a man with an eye for the main chance. He was
not content until he had introduced the art of ballet into the
public theatre. The first ballet to be played in public was
Pomone, for which not Lully but the contemporary composer
Robert Cambert wrote the music. This piece played for eight
months in Paris. Three years later it was staged in London. In
1681 the tradition that women dancers should not appear in the
public theatre was broken, and it was not long before the
ballerina began to win her place in the affections of the public.

Music often seems to be a man's world. So far as ballet is
concerned, however, the part played by women in shaping it has
been very considerable. Often they have brought to bear a
degree of common sense in which men may be found to be
lacking! In 1734 a famous Parisian dancer Mlle Sallé was
engaged to appear in London, in a ballet entitled *Pygmalion*.
Thinking to herself that she could neither show off her figure
nor her special skill to the best effect in the heavy costume she

had to wear in Paris, she wore only a simple dress of muslin, cut after the Grecian style. Some people appeared to be shocked; but most appreciated the change. Those who were given to debating aesthetic matters excused their enjoyment of the spectacle by pointing out that Mlle Sallé was doing the art of ballet a service by 'going back to nature'.

It is interesting that this dancer, who was brought into his opera season for 1734-5 inspired Handel to write the charming music for the ballet *Terpsichore* and the dances for the opera *Alcina*.

The esteem in which successful ballerinas were held in the eighteenth century is shown by the fine painting of Marie Anne Camargo by Nicholas Lancret, one of the famous French painters of the school of Watteau. Camargo, like Sallé, was sure that if ballet were to prosper then it depended a great deal on the commonsense of women. She shortened the length of skirts, introduced ballet slippers; invented new steps, and is said to have pioneered the wearing of tights. She became a leader of fashion, a boon to dress designers and shoe-makers, and something of legend in her lifetime. She was active throughout the second quarter of the eighteenth century.

When a great revival of interest began to develop in London some thirty years ago a new ballet society (out of which grew the Sadler's Wells and the later Royal Ballet) was named the Camargo Society, in memory of a great ballerina.

If the ballerinas moved towards a greater degree of naturalism on their own intuition it was not long before what they had begun stimulated theories. It so happened that the theories that emerged from the practice of these former stars of the ballet world happily fitted into theories which had developed in other contexts. The 'artificial' life of 'high society', as demonstrated in the courts of Europe, was seen as pointless, by certain writers. Among these was Jean-Jacques Rousseau, who pressed hard for a 'return to nature'.

The first stirrings of the Romantic Movement were beginning
to be experienced. A ballet-master of Paris, Jean Noverre, who
admired the music of Jean Philippe Rameau, published a treatise
in the form of *Letters on the Dance* in 1760, in which he put the
case for a simpler, more expressive, form of ballet that should be
in accordance with the presumed principles of classical dance.
A beautiful and expressive dance by Rameau stands at the head
of this chapter. In his Preface to *les Indes galantes,* from which
this is taken, the composer stated that, 'like the great Lully', he
took 'beautiful and simple nature as his model.' In contrast to the
'Zephyr' music, here is a vigorous dance for 'Savages' (Ex. 2.)

Ex.2

Opera and ballet, since both sprang from the same roots, have
at all times kept in contact with one another. The greatest opera
composer of the mid-eighteenth century was Willibald Gluck
(1714–87), a German-Bohemian by birth but since he worked
easily in different parts of Europe to be regarded as an international artist. He wrote operas in Italy in the approved Italian
style, and continued to exploit this style in opera houses in
England, Germany, Denmark, Bohemia and Austria. He became
the most celebrated composer in Vienna, where French plays,
French operas, and French ballets became fashionable just at the
time when Jean Noverre was laying down his principles for

ballet dancing. In 1760 Gluck composed music for a ballet, Don Juan, based on a play by Molière. This was a landmark in the history of ballet, for it departed from the idea that ballet should only exist in the world of 'make-believe' and startled audiences by its dramatic nature. The most exciting episode was a 'Dance of the Furies'.

Gluck was a reformer, and his wish to bring music and dramatic action closer together led to a new conception of opera. Gluck's greatest operas were *Orfeo & Euridice* (1762) and *Alceste* (1767). When *Orfeo* was produced in France in 1776 Gluck introduced the 'Dance of the Furies' from *Don Juan* between the first and second acts. Because Gluck broke away from the stiff and mechanical conventions of Italian opera he proved an inspiration to the great opera composers of the next generation. Of these the chief was Mozart, whose *Don Giovanni* owes something to Gluck's ballet on the same subject.

The Romantic period finally removed ballet from the narrow world of the Court and it became a popular art. Just as Italy had been the home of opera so France was regarded as the centre of ballet activity. Dancers, of whatever nationality, aspired to perform in Paris. One of the great Romantic dancers was the Italian-Swedish Marie Taglioni, whose technique of dancing on the tips of her toes (which required another revolution in footwear) gave to ballet the particular grace that remains its most admired characteristic. Taglioni's most famous rôle was that of the *Sylphide*.

One of the dancers who rivalled Taglioni in popular esteem was Fanny Elssler, whose father had been a close friend of and servant to Joseph Haydn – Fanny's godfather. In contrast to Taglioni – all lightness and delicacy – Elssler revelled in dramatic rôles.

In almost every department of music the name Bach appears. So far as ballet is concerned we look to Johann Sebastian's grandson, Wilhelm Friedrich Ernst Bach (1759–1845), who composed a 'Ballet-Pantomime' in Berlin in 1798. Two dances in particular suggest the atmosphere of Beethoven's 'Pastoral' Symphony (1807–8), which like all Beethoven's symphonies is affected by the spirit of the dance. Here the last of the male Bachs gives us a lively peasant dance (Ex. 3). Here, on the other hand, there is a more reflective expression of joy. (Ex. 4.) These pieces certainly 'take us back to nature'.

The love of ballet in France is reflected in some of the most popular works in the modern repertory. These include *Les Sylphides*, which is based on piano pieces composed by Frédéric Chopin, and the original scores of *Coppelia* (1870) and *Sylvia*

(1876) by Léo Delibes (1836–91). In his music Delibes showed
the lightness that belonged to the art of ballet as it was then
appreciated and this brought a new impulse into the art of
orchestration.

All modern French music may be said to have been influenced
by the national taste for ballet and the elements of grace, athletic
verve, and bright colouring, have proved a welcome counter
balance to the relative heaviness of other schools of orchestration.
Debussy's music is filled with a sense of freedom of movement
(look back at the example on page 110) and so is that of Maurice
Ravel (1875–1937), whose *Daphnis and Chloe* (1912) is one of
the most beautiful ballets of our time.

Like opera ballet has often exploited music for its own ends.
One may read an account of a performance where the composer's name is not even mentioned! The designer of a ballet
may seize a work by a composer (generally one who is dead so
as to avoid difficulties of copyright) and pull it about in order
to accommodate the talents of his ballet team. In this case
technique becomes an end in itself.

At the same time the art depends greatly on those who have
the imagination to perfect old and to develop new techniques.
Curiously, new techniques nearly always turn out to be variations on or expansions of old ideas.

Insofar as ballet is concerned there is, of course, only a single
'idea', of which at any period we see one or more particular
aspects. The 'idea' is to communicate through movement. Too
much concentration on technique as an end in itself makes this
aim unattainable.

One who tried to prevent ballet from being spoiled by too
much concentration on technical skill was the American dancer
Isadora Duncan (1878–1927). She attempted to recreate ballet
according to what she interpreted from the postures and costumes
which are all that remain of the art of dance of classical Greece.
At the same time she introduced movements which may be said

to have been 'natural' in that they imitated the movements of birds, and of waves in the sea. In a roundabout way ideas of this kind have had a good deal of effect in musical education.

'Music and movement' during the last thirty or forty years has taken its place in the curriculum of primary education. In general this has been based, though not directly, on the approach of Isadora Duncan. A more powerful influence, however, in this field has been that of Emile Jacques-Dalcroze (1865–1950), a Swiss musician and educationist who was a pupil of Delibes in Paris. Dalcroze did important pioneer work and in developing the art of free expression through movement enabled many children to gain a new sense of musical understanding. Not only has the work of Dalcroze affected education but it has also left its mark on the promise of medicine. Music and movement is now much used as an aid to restoring sick people to health, and also as a means of encouraging those who are described as mentally retarded.

This sounds a far cry from ballet. And it is a long way from the refined art of a Fonteyn to the modest, often crude, exercises of small children in a village school or of pupils in a 'handicapped centre'. But it is only by realising that what we call ballet is so deeply rooted in human behaviour that we can begin to understand what it is about.

The power of ballet can release the genius of one composer just as the power of words can release that of another. As always the composer needs incentive. Earlier on we referred to the ballet music of Stravinsky – undoubtedly the greatest ballet composer of this century. But Stravinsky would not have written the music of *The Firebird* (1910), *Petrushka* (1911), *The Rite of Spring*, and other works of similar nature, without the tradition that had grown up in Russia and without the inspiration of Sergei Diaghilev (1872–1929).

Ballet, after the French manner, was introduced into Russia by Peter the Great, who wished to 'westernize' the Russian way of life. The art developed through the eighteenth and nineteenth centuries to culminate in the great ballet scores of Tchaikovsky, whose *Swan Lake* (1877), *Sleeping Beauty* (1890), and *The Nutcracker* (1892) are classics of ballet music. While these works of Tchaikovsky are now regarded as amongst the greatest of their kind, it is worth remembering that they were looked at with great suspicion when first produced. They were, it was said, too much like symphonic music and there was too little scope for the kind of virtuoso dancing that was appreciated in Moscow and St Petersburg.

Diaghilev, an expert in painting as well as in music, worked closely with the great dancer Mikhail Fokin. Between them they reformed dancing techniques on the one hand and decided that the art could only become an effective part of twentieth century culture if skilled composers could be persuaded to spare some of their talents to this end. Stravinsky is an example of the right composer arriving at the right time. He understood what Diaghilev was striving for and that the Russian-motivated music of Tchaikovsky, Borodin and Rimsky-Korsakov was the point from which the project should be approached.

Stravinsky's ballet music reaches back to the moods expressed through folk-music, beyond that to the ideas out of which all ritual-dance comes, yet remains true to its own age. Stravinsky's ballet music was once regarded as 'modern'. It is now placed among the classical works of the twentieth century. We may say that Stravinsky's music 'moves with the times'. This is not in itself important. What is important is that it moves. This is the lesson that the musician learns from ballet.

XI

Comic Opera

G.B. Pergolesi, "La serva padrona"

Serpina

Mi per-cuo - te, mi per-cuo-te Il mar-tel-lin d'a-mo-re
(*It strikes me —   the little hammer of love,*

Uberto

Che?   Ma
(*What?   But*

T HE easiest way to describe comedy is to say that it makes
us laugh. What makes us laugh generally (though not
always) concerns the less serious side of life. So far so good.
But what is the less serious side of life, and what is it that, when
it occurs, makes us laugh?

We laugh at the antics of a clown in the circus. This we do
because he behaves differently from us; because his absurdities
make us feel more certain that as we are not like him we are
'normal'. Some clowns, of course, have the genius to make us
realise that their behaviour is after all not so far removed from
our own; that each one of us has something of the clown in him.

The films of Laurel and Hardy show another form of clown-
ing. Much of their comedy is slapstick and consists of actions that
seem to be funny because they are anti-social. Such comedy has
in it the idea of dissatisfaction, of rebellion. The famous films of
Charles Chaplin have something of the same quality, but since
Chaplin in particular always appears to be a victim of situations –
a little, inoffensive man up against heavy odds – we laugh with
him rather more than at him.

Certain actions, perhaps, make us laugh most of all, because
our easiest way of expressing ourselves and understanding the
expression of others is through doing so.

Words may quickly move us to laughter. An unusual arrangement of words can do this. A misprint, which is quite accidental,
appears as funny. So does the misuse of words as made familiar
by Mrs Malaprop, in Sheridan's *The Rivals*.

In drawing or painting opportunities for suggesting what is
purely comic are fewer than in actions or through the use – or
misuse – of words. But caricature, the most obvious medium, can
exert a powerful effect. The great caricaturist relies on exaggera-
tion, but also on simplicity. The most famous political cartoonists
have often made statesmen familiar through emphasis on one
characteristic oddity.

By itself music is the least likely of the arts to cause laughter.
We may laugh at a quick tune played on, say, the tuba, but
only because it is odd that such a weighty instrument should
attempt the feat. Here, however, it is not the music that is
comic, but the situation. That is the case with Haydn's 'Farewell'
Symphony – in the last movement of which the players pack up
their music and instruments and go one by one until only a
single violinist is left; then he departs. Occasionally one may
hear some such songs as 'Little Polly Flinders', *in the style of
Handel*. This is parody. It is a copy of a style, but the style is
applied to new and usually inappropriate conditions. We may
or may not find it amusing.

That music has a place in the field of humour is shown, however, by the long line of comic operas. It is significant that it is really only when music is associated with words and with actions that it can help in raising laughter.

Comedy springs from what is near at hand. It centres on contrasts, and sometimes on the bringing together of opposites. Comedy shows the accidents and the oddities of life. Comedy looks at the world as it is and then sees it seemingly turned upside down. Therefore, while it usually does not go far away for its basic material, it can, in the hands of a fine artist, take us into a realm of fantasy or improbability. This is the art of James Thurber, and of Danny Kaye.

Since parody is one part of comedy, the master of comedy, in whatever medium he works, can hold up people or situations to ridicule. Comic artists have not always been popular with authority. Comic plays and comic operas have sometimes been banned. It is not so long ago that a celebrated satirical programme on British television was taken off because it gave offence. Just over two hundred years previously John Gay's ballad opera *Polly* was banned. The government of the day was afraid of ridicule. John Gay had already enjoyed enormous success with *The Beggar's Opera*, one of the most important of all 'comic' stage pieces.

We must go behind this work, which was first produced in 1728, and discover how the idea of music and comedy in combination emerged.

As has been shown the origins of most art-forms familiar to us can be seen in folk-art. The dumb-show, the mime, the masquerade, all had the seeds of one sort of comedy, for they frequently illustrated what was grotesque. In the religious drama of the Middle Ages when shepherds or sailors were introduced they were treated as figures of fun. The idea that the 'common' people were funny was established very early by people of higher social standing. We may still hear this idea sometimes expressed, and where we do we may notice how it usually stems from a sense of fear. So, people who speak with a 'cultured' accent (this applies in almost all 'civilised' countries) think that those who do not are to be laughed at. Sometimes, of course, this may apply in reverse.

The earliest of European dramas that are still performed deal in large measure with characters of noble birth. This is made clear by the principal characters of any Shakespearean plays. The earliest operas went one better. They took as heroes or heroines the stock figures of Greek mythology – for reasons which have been shown.

Human nature being what it is, however, the need for relaxation from serious thought is always present. The patrons of the seventeenth-century theatre were all in favour of culture (not for its own sake but because it redounded to their credit to show a fashionable interest; but they also relished, and expected, more light-hearted diversion.

To the ends of acts of plays – this was true of those of Shakespeare – separate, short, entertainments were added. In the case of the English theatre these were known as Jigs, dances (as the title suggests) extended into some kind of story. The extended Jig dealt invariably with some familiar 'low-life' character and his adventures. The Jig was the Elizabethan counterpart, perhaps, to the comic strip cartoon of today; neither more nor less important.

When 'serious opera' (*opera seria*) was well established it became a convention to put something corresponding to the English Jig in between the acts. (Something of the effect on the audience may be understood from the advertisements shown between the parts of a serious play on television.) This interlude, or *intermezzo*, usually borrowed two familiar figures from popular drama : the old man (a bass singer) – who could be made to look ridiculous in many ways – and the maid-servant, with whom he would inevitably fall in love. This situation gave

a good deal of scope – this is the advantage of simple situations –
interpretation of it could range from slapstick comedy to
near-tragedy.

One composer of genius turned this *intermezzo* into an
important and independent form of its own. This was Giovanni
Battista Pergolesi (1710–36). In 1733 he was commissioned to
write an intermezzo for a theatre in Naples to be incidental to a
serious opera, *The Proud Prisoner*. The intermezzo was called
La serva padrona (*The servant as mistress*). The serious opera
was soon forgotten : the comic interlude remained and may still
frequently be heard.

The first performance of *La serva padrona* took place in the
Theatre of St Bartholomew in Naples, on August 28, 1733. The
story is as simple as can be; it merely tells how the servant girl
Serpina, having made up her mind to do so, so captivated her
elderly employer, Uberto, that he in the end made her his wife.
In the period in which the piece was composed this was an
incongruous situation. That sort of thing did not happen. Or
did it? If it did, then it shouldn't.

In contrast to the conventions of serious opera here were no
figures out of the history-book, but lively, familiar, everyday
persons. When the librettist and the musician had dealt with
them they became a little stylised; but they were recognisable –
and to be laughed at. The girl was amusing because she was
cheeky. The old man because he was stripped of his pretensions.
The *intermezzo* was entertaining; but it showed a good deal
that was familiar in human behaviour. Pergolesi brought opera
a little nearer to reality as it is generally understood.

Comedy depends a great deal on contrast. The heroine of the
intermezzo was a high soprano, the hero (or the villain) a bass.
In this kind of entertainment the bass was featured more than in
opera of a serious kind. Pergolesi's music not only aimed at
being popular, it was popular. This was due to its lightness and
tunefulness, to the zest with which melody flew along over

slender orchestration and barely noticeable harmony. In general the composer of the period aimed at lightness and elegance so that it was perhaps inevitable that a distinctively 'comic' style of music should develop.

Some of the terms used in respect of comic opera have (you may have noticed) also been applied to ballet. Between these two branches of art there is a connection. This connection is rhythm. Both ballet and comic opera depend on quickness of movement, changes of metre, clarity in musical accent, and economy in the use of musical notes. The relationship between the modern 'musical' and dance idiom shows this quite as clearly as any historical work.

Although other composers had previously introduced *inter-mezzi* into operas it was Pergolesi's *La serva Padrona* that really gave to this form a sense of purpose and independence. Pergolesi was not merely content to be comic in a superficial way. His wonderful melodic gift, his sense of timing, and the manner in which he showed both the outer and inner qualities of his characters, all enabled audiences to appreciate the values of a fully rounded musical comedy. The qualities of Pergolesi's comedy-through-music (if we may so call it) are summed up in the duet extract at the beginning of the chapter.

After the production of *La serva padrona* two terms were made familiar in respect of opera. On the one hand there was *opera seria*, on the other *opera buffa*. Pergolesi's work went into the repertoires of travelling companies. In 1738 it was performed in Parma. A year later it was given at Graz, in Austria, and also in a theatre near Bologna. In 1740 performances took place in Venice, Dresden, and Munich, and the year afterwards in the Haymarket Theatre, in London. It swept Europe with all the velocity of a present-day commercial success, and in 1790 received its American premiere, in Baltimore.

La serva padrona was performed in Paris for the first time in 1746. Six years later it was revived in Paris and then it was the cause of a bitter quarrel. By this time a French tradition of serious opera had been established through the works of Lully and Jean-Philippe Rameau. Of this tradition the French intellectuals were proud, and it was felt that *La serva padrona* and all that it stood for was a bad influence, because cheapening, both in music and drama. Besides, it was Italian. On the other hand there were many who approved the lightness and gaiety of Pergolesi's style and were prepared to defend it. Not only were there demonstrations by the rival supporters, but numerous booklets and pamphlets were written, in defence of one or the other side. The row between the rival gangs in the 'War of buffoons' as it was called was as acrimonious as that which nowadays often flares up between the supporters of opposing football teams.

La serva padrona became one of the most popular of all operas. It was translated into many languages and accepted not as an Italian opera but as a universal symbol of the comic spirit in music. As will be seen comedy through music often tends to be seen in a more local light. Pergolesi himself, after a life of relative poverty and near obscurity, hardly enjoyed the success of his work. He died at the age of twenty-six and was buried in a pauper's grave.

The *opera buffa* composer aimed to get on terms with his audience at once. This meant that the music should be direct and uncomplicated. It should therefore have something of the quality of folk-song. The nearer to folk-song and to the character of the folk-song singer – that is, the 'peasant' class – musical dramas approach the more entertaining they will appear to persons who consider themselves of higher social or intellectual standing. In the year 1732 Pergolesi had composed an intermezzo in which the servants were drawn direct from Neapolitan life, singing in the Neapolitan dialect and to melodies borrowed from local folk-tradition.

The value of folk-song in establishing a sense of comedy was better appreciated in the eighteenth century than in later times. The contrast between the uneducated and the educated in what was known as an 'Age of Enlightenment' was strongly felt. But there were those who could handle the element of comedy that was proposed in this way with sympathy. We rightly do not consider Johann Sebastian Bach as a master of comic opera; because he never had the opportunity to compose opera. But he certainly had a strong feeling for comedy. This should not surprise us, for it is impossible to be a great creative artist without possessing such a feeling.

In Bach's case this shows up in its most attractive form in the so-called *Peasant Cantata,* a piece written for a local festival in honour of a squire (whose name no longer matters). Here Bach made use of the Leipzig dialect that marked his own speech, and he introduced on the one hand local folk-tunes and on the other (to make fun of the 'city' folk) delicate music in a French idiom. In our own time we find Kodály making a similar contrast, between Hungarian folk-music and a classical French idiom, in the folk-opera *Háry János.* Another piece by Bach that is not only comic, but, in a light-hearted way, also critical – of modishness and fashion – is the *Coffee Cantata.*

Many German composers learned at that time to write in the Italian style – for this was thought of as a general style suitable for musical ideas anywhere. But, as in the case of Bach and Handel, the style was modified by German inflections. Georg Philipp Telemann was a contemporary of Handel and Bach and a very successful composer indeed. He was versatile and equally at home in symphonic and chamber music as in oratorio and opera. He was a quick worker and an opportunist, and ready to try his hand at any commission. An intermezzo by him, on a similar story to that of *La serva padrona* was produced in Hamburg in 1725. This was called *Pimpinone.* In this work the characterisation is shrewd and in certain respects anticipated that of Mozart. Telemann, like Mozart, was skilful in showing contrasts of character in musical ensemble – duets, trios, quartets. A further work by Telemann to illustrate another line of comic development, stemming from literature, is *The Patient Socrates*. In this gay, lively, tuneful work we find the composer dealing with a satirical text written by a typical author of the period – Johann Ulrich von König. By a variety of musical means – through the effective use of recitative and aria and by near-quotes from folk-song – Telemann achieves a truly comic, often satirical, feeling.

Side by side with these works there are also to be found in eighteenth century Germany and Austria the play-on-a-local-subject-with-folk-tune that was termed *Singspiel*. In due course all the separate items of German and Italian opera were drawn together into the great operas of Mozart.

In England there was also a long tradition of play with music. Shakespeare's plays, of course, were a part of this tradition in that music played a not unimportant part in them. And sometimes Shakespeare required popular songs or ballads of the day to be introduced. A vivid picture in *The Winter's Tale* gives us an insight into the country-music of those days as Autolycus comes with his ballads. Across the years ballads accumulated and one could hardly visit an English theatre during the seventeenth and eighteen centuries without hearing many ballads sung. Sometimes before plays or during intervals, but often as part of the play.

It was in the year 1728 that John Gay, the poet, had the idea of stringing a whole series of ballads together into one 'opera'. But this was to be no ordinary opera. Indeed it was thought up as a parody on the Italian opera that had invaded London – to the displeasure of many. If 'serious opera' dealt with 'high life', then Gay determined to write a work that dealt with 'low life'. In a moment of inspiration he hit upon the right title – *The Beggars' Opera*.

Earlier on it was suggested that the typical *opera buffa* story was similar to a 'comic strip' cartoon. The characters of *The Beggars' Opera* would also come up well in cartoon treatment. But these are rough-necks, and their records, if shown in a modern mass-circulation paper, would cause a good deal of head-shaking.

The names of the characters belong to the more realistic parts of English fiction – to those shown, for instance, in the novels of Daniel Defoe and Henry Fielding – rather than the rarified world of Italian opera. Here are some of them : Peachum, Lockit, Macheath (a name made much use of in English political satire at the present time), Filch, Jemmy Twitcher, Crookfinger'd Jack . . . Lucy Lockit (who side-stepped into a nursery rhyme), Mrs Vixen, Mrs Slammekin, Molly Brazen . . . a motley collection of thieves, highwaymen, crooks, and (as they are called) 'women of the town'.

John Gay, an acquaintance of Handel, wrote the story. Why did he do so? First, because he was, like many of his colleagues who were interested in the theatre, fed up with the way in which the wealthiest and therefore most influential patrons of the theatre clamoured for Italian opera. Second, because of the overbearing manner of many of the Italian opera stars. Third, because he resented the easy money that was going into the wrong pockets, to the great disadvantage of native actors and singers. Fourth, because he did not like the government led by Sir Robert Walpole, criticism of which was more possible and more effective through the indirect medium of satirical comedy. Fifth, because he was both repelled and attracted by the criminal life of London and which in any case he saw as a vivid theme for dramatic treatment.

The Beggars' Opera was staged at the theatre in Lincoln's Inn Fields managed by John Rich, on January 29, 1728. The audience immediately recognised that Macheath was a parody of Walpole. The rivalry between Polly Peacham and Lucy Lockit was an entertaining skit on the celebrated *prima donna* feud between two of Handel's singers, Francesca Cuzzoni and Faustina Bordoni. The series opera of the day invariably included a 'prison scene'. So too did *The Beggars' Opera*, but in this the scene was laid in Newgate, not in some imagined fortress of the classical past. The audience relished the language of the dialogue – direct, often rude, but with a cutting edge of wit. Then there was the music.

The division between serious and popular music is by no means only one that is recognised in our own time. In eighteenth century England there was the music of the opera-house and the drawing-room on the one hand and the music of the streets, the taverns, and the pleasure-gardens on the other. To the first category belonged the Italian, or Italian inspired, aria, cantata, and sonata; to the second the often scurrilous and always topical ballad. Many of these ballads – published on single sheets – were of a political nature; there are a large number, for example, which illustrate the division of political thought into Tory and Whig.

Ballads were not vaguely allusive country pieces, but hard-hitting, critical, commentaries on everyday affairs. The tunes of the ballads were simple and singable. They had to be. They were popular because they were easy to sing and to remember and also because of the ideas which they carried. This is always true of popular tunes: their popularity depends not on any special musical merit, but on the association of the music with something outside of music.

John Gay appreciated that by threading a set of popular tunes through his story he could make a double appeal to his audience. The principle that the public will pay to hear what it likes is a sound one. In the case of *The Beggars' Opera* it worked to perfection.

So far as popular tunes are concerned Gay had a wide field to choose from. In those days popular tunes lived longer than they appear to do today. Some of the tunes, like *Greensleeves*,

were popular in Elizabethan times. Gay's selection takes us back
in time. Not only does it include sixteenth century melodies but
also some of the most famous of Henry Purcell's airs – such as
'Britons strike home', from the patriotic opera *King Arthur*
(see page 123). Gay also chose melodies composed by other
conspicuous composers of the English school, notably John
Eccles and Jeremiah Clarke. These composers, like Purcell, were
equally at home in the departments of 'light' and 'serious' music,
and they did a great deal to bridge the gap. The most famous
composer of the day was, of course, Handel. Handel's most
celebrated opera was *Rinaldo*. So a noble march from *Rinaldo*
is found in *The Beggars' Opera*, with these words :

> Let us take the Road.
> Hark ! I hear the sound of coaches !
> The hour of Attack approaches,
> To your Arms, brave Boys, and load.
>
> See the Ball I hold !
> Let the Chymists tail like Asses,
> Our Fire their Fire surpasses,
> And turns all our lead to Gold.

The Gang (reads the stage direction that follows), *rang'd in the
Front of the stage, load their Pistols, and stick them under their
Girdles; then go off singing the first part in chorus.*

There were many ballads that were popular in London from,
or about, the Welsh, the Scottish, the Irish. Gay drew on all
these sources. Once or twice he looked at the image of French
culture; just as Bach did in the *Peasant Cantata*, and we find
French tunes in *The Beggars' Opera*. One of them – set by Gay
as a drinking song – is familiar to us in another guise – as a
Christmas carol ! As has already been seen *The Beggars' Opera*
affected the world of music for children. Class-teachers of today

would not be teaching 'Over the hills and far away' and 'Gossip Joan' except that these airs had been popularised in *The Beggars' Opera*.

In arranging the musical side of the work Gay was grateful for the help of John Christopher Pepusch (1667–1752), a German musician who had been living in England since about 1700.

Gay designed a sequel to *The Beggars' Opera*. The text of this, entitled *Polly*, was published in 1729. But *Polly* was not performed until almost half a century later. In his Preface Gay explained how he had fallen foul of authority. The situation that arose is not unfamiliar in modern times. Indeed, we are reminded once again how the artist is at all times liable to be regarded with suspicion.

' 'Twas on Saturday morning December 7th, 1728', wrote Gay, 'that I waited upon the Lord Chamberlain; I desir'd to have the honour of reading the Opera to his Grace, but he order'd me to leave it with him, which I did upon expectation of having it return'd on the Monday following, but I had it not 'till Thursday December 12, when I receiv'd it from his Grace with this answer; that it was not allow'd to be acted, but commanded to be supprest. This was told me in general without any reasons assign'd or any charge against me of my having given any particular offence.'

Gay was later told that he had been guilty of writing many 'libels and seditious pamphlets', and 'immoralities'.

After that time there was a long record of censorship of operas, on political grounds. This has persisted to the present day. One comic opera that had to slide round the censor was Mozart's *Marriage of Figaro*. This was because the play by Pierre Beaumarchais, on which the libretto was based, was regarded in Austria as seditious. The reason for this was that servants made fun of their masters. This tendency, however, lies deep in the tradition of comedy : indeed it is, perhaps, in a way what comedy is about.

YG

From this we may conclude that comic opera can be very serious; but serious in a different way from 'serious opera'. The composer of comic opera, in relation to the composer of 'serious opera' looks at the connection between words and music, or plot and music, from another standpoint. In comic opera the balance is tilted a little away from music and towards words and action. It requires great experience, however, to judge the degree at which the balance should be tilted. In modern times the wittiest operas (or rather operettas) are those by William Gilbert and Arthur Sullivan, in which the institutions of Victorian England were held up and subjected to humourously critical scrutiny. That they had no successors is an indication of the rarity with which the comic music brings together librettist and musician into a working partnership.

XII
Wagner & Music Drama

THE nineteenth century often seems the great age of optimism. For the first time in history the immense possibilities of technological development, as affecting the quality of the lives of the majority rather than the minority, became apparent. The British people, firmly based on their old traditions and on the resources of a vast overseas empire, prospered, and as wealth accumulated from the ever increasing factories of the north a golden future seemed assured. In Europe the highest degree of industrialisation took place in Germany, especially in the Ruhr and in central Saxony.

Unlike the British, however, the Germans had no assured

line of tradition, nor was their political unity certain. Neverthe-less, still smarting from the damage caused throughout Germany by the armies of Napoleon at the beginning of the century, and inspired by a sense of recent achievement in many fields of culture, the leaders of Germany looked with confidence to the time when their country would be the most important in Europe.

In some respects Germany during the nineteenth century was the most important nation in Europe. Her philosophers – among whom were Immanuel Kant, Johann Fichte, Georg Hegel, and Friedrich Nietzsche, were the most influential in the whole field of philosophy. Her poets and dramatists, in particular Johann Wolfgang von Goethe, Johann Schiller, and Heinrich Heine, built up a great body of literature that represents a classical era in world literature.

Both philosophers and poets were deeply concerned with the senses by which man first acquires knowledge of the world. They were also concerned with man's emotional behaviour, by the responses of human feelings, by the relationships between man and man, man and woman, and man and nature. It is not surprising that under these circumstances music, which among the arts most clearly reflects feelings and appeals to the emotions, took an important place.

The condition of an art at any one time and in any one place is the result of history in its many forms. For centuries German composers, responding to their own impulses, to their patrons, and to the general climate of thought, developed the emotional significance of music. At the same time (and this is paralleled by progress in other fields) they worked hard at a scientific and theoretical aspects of music. It has long been a convention for others to say that the Germans take their music 'seriously'.

The most obvious case is that of Johann Sebastian Bach, whose power to move us by the appeal to the emotions but also by his mastery of formal design is almost unsurpassed. From the time of Bach until the middle of the nineteenth century German composers increasingly came to dominate musical thought.

The row of great composers of German birth or education is impressive. We remember the sons of Bach, the early makers of the symphony who worked at the Court of Mannheim, Mozart (of German extraction, though born in Salzburg), Haydn (Austro-Hungarian, but German-speaking), Beethoven, Schubert (Austrian, but the master of German song), Weber, Mendelssohn, Schumann. . . .

If you listen to music by those composers in that order you will begin to appreciate that a striking feature of that music is its apparently increasing effectiveness in giving information – through descriptive, or programme techniques – on the one hand, and in seeming to uncover fresh emotional patterns within the language of music on the other. That composers had this as their aim is shown by an increasing use of descriptive titles for pieces, and even by the use of more or less descriptive terms for giving directions to the performer about the expression to be introduced into interpretation.

There was a magnificent musical tradition in Germany. The great composers had appeared not because of some magical and disproportionate bestowal of genius, but because music was cultivated and valued at every level of society. In the course of time the musical tradition became the theme of a conscious national veneration. The biographies of composers written at the beginning of the nineteenth century – the most notable being that of Bach by Johann Forkel, published in 1802 – were largely inspired by a sense of national duty.

Certain points now begin to emerge with clarity. Music in Germany had become a national symbol, providing a recognis-able and long tradition, a unique medium through which feelings and hopes could be expressed, and a reflection of the world. Beethoven's 'Eroica' symphony was the record of the life of the 'hero'. The 'Pastoral' symphony was intended to show the inter-

dependence of man and nature. The 'Choral' symphony was a
notable demonstration of nineteenth century optimism, and a
declaration of faith in the ultimate ability of men to live together
in peace. These were key works. In a sense they still are, for they
are as regular in performance today as they ever were.

One of the ideas that inspired the Romantic composer of the
nineteenth century was that which suggested that music could in
some ways do as well as, or even better than, any other art in
the matter of description. It may not be the job of the composer
to describe; the music-lover, however, is more often than not
ready to believe that it should be. What, he says, is the music
about? Some forms of music help to strengthen this belief more
than others. None more than opera – the whole purpose of
which is to convey information.

During the eighteenth century the most popular composers of
opera were Italian. Towards the end of the century a strong
reaction set in in Germany. Operas, it was said, should be based
on German ideas, and the texts should be in the German
language. Mozart's *The Magic Flute*, first produced in Vienna
in 1791, was a turning-point. Here at last was a great opera that
was German rather than Italian.

Thirty years after the first production of *The Magic Flute*
Carl Maria von Weber's *Der Freischütz* (The Marksman) was
produced in Berlin. This romance, set in the woodlands of
Germany, picturing the kind of country life that was idealised by
Germans in the nineteenth century and by foreign tourists ever
since, and full of magic and mystery, was another major step
forward in the establishment of a national opera.

Weber was the nephew of Mozart's wife. He was a family
friend of the Wagner family.

Richard Wagner was born in Leipzig in 1813 at a time when
the Napoleonic campaign in Germany was reaching its climax.
The Battle of Leipzig, in which the French forces were defeated,
took place a few months after Wagner's birth. The effect of this

victory was very great. It was not possible for a boy to grow up in Leipzig – indeed in Germany – without feeling a special sense of national pride.

Wagner's family background was literary, and his uncle Adolf was a distinguished scholar, who revered Goethe and had personally known Schiller. Richard Wagner later acknowledged how much he was indebted to his uncle's taste and knowledge. His father died when he was an infant and his mother re-married. Wagner's stepfather, Ludwig Geyer, was an actor, with some skill in painting. Richard's early interest in the theatre was strengthened by his enthusiasm for Weber's *Der Freischütz*, by frequently meeting people connected with the theatre, and by the fact that two of his sisters became actresses.

One of these sisters married Friedrich Brockhaus, one of the most important of German publishers. Because of this Wagner's opportunities for studying literature – already stimulated by the excellent teaching of the school he attended in Leipzig – were increased.

As for music Richard learned the piano and went to concerts and operas. In Leipzig the orchestral concerts were famous. Wagner heard the symphonies of Beethoven. These made a profound impression on him. He was also deeply stirred by Beethoven's opera *Fidelio*, by Mozart's *Requiem Mass*, and by the romantic operas of Heinrich Marschner (1795–1861).

As a young man Marschner knew Beethoven, who advised him to compose sonatas and symphonic music in order to perfect his already considerable technical skills. He did not follow this advice; but it was the principle of the symphony that was to determine the structure of Wagner's music. Marschner had his own contribution to make to Wagner's development. He understood the tone-colours of the orchestra as well as any of his contemporaries, and thus developed a distinctively descriptive style. Distinctive because he specialised in depicted nature in its various aspects and the supernatural forces, represented by 'apparitions', that were thought sometimes to lie behind nature.

Richard Wagner was a schoolboy in Leipzig when Marschner, Director of the Opera-house in the city, produced his most famous work – *The Vampyr* – in 1828. In his autobiography Wagner tells what a great impression the performance of this work by the opera company from Dresden made on him. A year later he was impressed, in a different way, by Marschner's *The Knight Templar and the Jewess*. This was based on *Ivanhoe* by Walter Scott, a writer whose romantic and historical stories were read avidly all over Europe.

Marschner left Leipzig to become Director of the Opera in Hanover, and in 1833 he produced *Hans Heiling*, another very popular work, with a story calculated to appeal to those with a taste for the fantastic and horrific. There are many people today who share this same taste – but they read space fiction and the works of Ian Fleming. The point is made so that the tendency in opera represented by Wagner and Marschner can be seen in perspective: what they stood for was something that lies deep and permanent in human nature. In those days, and in that country, opera was the obvious and popular medium for its expression.

There were two other German composers whose operas helped to establish a national type of opera. One was Ludwig Spohr (1784–1859), who had been an occasional paying-guest in the Wagner household during Richard's boyhood. His most important opera was on the subject of *Faust*, a legend that exercised a particular fascination for German composers. The other was Albert Lortzing (1801–51), a genial composer with a rich sense of comedy. In Lortzing's *Czar and Carpenter* (1837), which is still in the operatic repertoire, we see how a composer of very great talent could treat a historical story – in this case about Peter the Great, of Russia – with such understanding that the past could appear as though in the present. Of his later operas

The Poacher (1842) and *The Armourer* (1846) show a keen insight into the relationship between music and nature, and, again, that between the present and the past.

The hazards of being an artist with progressive ideas in a politically reactionary society were shown in Lortzing's case by the fact that in 1848 he found it impossible to stage one of his operas. This, *Regina*, dealt with the subject of revolution, and because it was treated in a 'liberal' manner was too hot for any producer who wished to keep his place to touch. In 1848 liberalism was suspect, for the rulers of the German States were in the middle of suppressing a spate of revolution. Spohr also knew what it was to be penalised for his political views. His radical tendencies, of which he made no secret, brought him into frequent conflict with his employer, the ruler of Hesse.

Weber, Marschner, Spohr, and Lortzing made a strong quartet of composers. Between them they showed how opera could be made to mean something to German audiences by giving the music a local flavour, and by developing a new kind of dramatic expression within music. When we speak of the dramatic element of music we think of this as being realistic. Orchestration is the most obvious manner of suggesting what is real. These German composers, all strongly impressed by Beethoven, developed a new style or orchestration. In so doing they made the orchestra not merely an accompaniment *to* the voice (which it was regarded as in the standard Italian operas of the period) but also a partner *with* the voice. In another sphere Franz Schubert developed this idea of partnership, with the piano equalling the voice in importance in his songs.

In *Faust* Spohr tried to unify the opera by using brief, but descriptive themes to show the nature of his characters. The theory was that the listener having once heard a theme would have his attention turned in the right direction when the same theme should be repeated. In the opera *Undine* (1845) Lortzing made use of this principle. The technique, centred on the use of

a significant and descriptive theme, gave a new word to the
vocabulary of music : *Leitmotiv*, meaning 'leading theme'. This
seems a far cry from the early opera of the Florentines described
in Chapter 8; because the music of the nineteenth century seems
not only to be more important than words, but to be doing their
work. Yet when Richard Wagner turned his full attention to
opera he intended to restore the situation so that the ideal of
opera was once again as it formerly had been.

Deeply concerned about the reputation of German literature
and German music, Wagner tried his hand at romantic fiction,
poetry, and drama, on the one hand, and symphonic music on
the other. Finding more and more, however, that the theatre
absorbed his interest, Wagner determined to canalise his many
enthusiasms in the one art that could take them all : the opera.

Fortunately it was not difficult for him to find work. His
brother Albert held an appointment in the theatre in Würzburg
and he managed to arrange that Richard should be engaged as
a temporary chorus-master. After a spell at Würzburg, Wagner
was fortunate in being given the musical direction of the charming little theatre (built by Goethe) in the watering-place of
Bad Lauchstädt, near to Halle. Both here (where a plaque in
the orchestra reminds us that Wagner once worked in the
theatre) and at Würzburg Wagner gained invaluable experience
of operatic and theatrical techniques. He had to adapt himself to
the resources of these not very important theatres, to be able to
arrange items and to compose additional items in a short space
of time. He learned the hard way.

In 1833 he moved on with the company that had been
stationed at Bad Lauchstädt to the city of Magdeburg. From
Magdeburg he went to Königsberg, and from Königsberg to the
Baltic port of Riga. His next assignment was at Dresden in 1842.
Here, in a famous opera-house, he felt that he had found his
feet, for he was the deputy musical director, with much responsibility and, he hoped, many opportunities.

But in 1849 Wagner was an exile from Dresden, and from Germany. Involvement in the political upheaval of 1848 on the revolutionary side had put him wrong with the authorities. Had he stayed in Germany he would have been arrested. So he took refuge in Switzerland.

In the meanwhile he had been coming to terms with himself as a composer. In spite of disappointments and disapproving noises from critics he had indeed established himself as a composer of individuality.

We may see how he picked up the ideas that were already in the air. Aged nineteen he had attempted first a novel and then an opera libretto (full of mystery, terror, and sudden death) called *The Marriage*. The exercise convinced him that if he should ever compose an opera it could only be to the libretto of his own. *The Marriage* was put aside and he composed another libretto – *The Fairies* – which also had many of the ingredients to be found in German dramatic and operatic literature of that time. He wrote music for *The Fairies* in what he called 'a German style'. In spite of the fact that he was unable to have this piece performed Wagner persisted. His next essay in opera, *The Ban on Love*, was based on Shakespeare's *Measure for Measure*.

After much effort *The Ban on Love* was produced in Magdeburg on March 29, 1836. To say that this was a failure would be an understatement. It was a catastrophe, and Wagner was glad to leave Magdeburg.

The years passed, and Wagner's mind settled on other ideas. He spent some time in London and in Paris. A popular play of the time in London was *Rienzi*, adapted from a novel by Bulwer Lytton. Wagner had read the novel and was fired by this patriotic tale of fourteenth-century Rome. He saw that the hope of Rienzi that Rome should be freed from the tyrannic rule of a small group of arrogant noblemen, given a better form of government, and ultimately lead the world overlapped his own ideals – and those of many of his countrymen – regarding Germany. He appreciated that the plot, with its setting amid the famous buildings of Rome, was natural for dramatic treatment on a large scale. Further, since he hoped for success in Paris he realised that it would be wise to write a spectacular opera in the manner of Giacomo Meyerbeer (1791–1864). Meyerbeer had popularised opera by his skill in bringing plots to life through the vivid quality of his orchestration.

A composer rarely works on one project exclusively. His mind is always full of the works he wishes to compose, and one idea sets others in motion. When he had sailed to London in 1839 Wagner had talked with the seamen who worked the ship, the *Thetis*, in which he travelled. They told him the legend of the Flying Dutchman – who was condemned by the Devil forever to sail the seas unless he should, in visiting land once in every seven years, find a woman who would love him and save him from his fate. This suited his mystical sense and he set to work to write a libretto for an opera.

Other stories that he came across included those of Tannhäuser, and of Lohengrin, knightly figures of medieval Germany whose adventures, misfortunes, love-stories, religious beliefs, strongly attracted the Germans of the Romantic era. Wagner not only recognised that these legends provided marvellous subjects for opera, but appreciated that by exposing them through the medium of operatic music he could also give new insights into human nature. This, after all, was the deliberate purpose of the Romantic composer. The abiding popularity of Wagner, both in opera-house and concert-hall, is due to this. He more than any composer of his age, with the exception of Verdi, appears to show the nature and pattern of the feelings that may not be expressed so truthfully through any other idiom.

We have discussed 'programme music', that is music which is descriptive in intention. Wagner wrote 'programme music' because a theatre composer can hardly do otherwise. But such music deals with the *outside* of ideas. A 'hero' can be shown by conventionally 'heroic' music, orchestrated in a way which leads us to understand that it is 'heroic'. Any composer can work on this level, as the scores that accompany most films and television plays will indicate. What we want music to do, however, is to tell us not that a man is a saint, or a hero, or a villain; but what *kind* of saint, hero, or villain, he is.

Wagner knew that no man is to be put in one class exclusively. He knew that every man is a mixture, of good and bad, of fear and courage, of faith and lack of faith. He knew too that what a man is depends on those with whom he lives, most of all on his relationship with those nearest to him. Wagner knew all this from his own experience of life (his biography is as complicated and as absorbing as that of any of his operatic characters), and also from his wide reading. Wagner was not only interested in what people were, but in how they became what they were, and how they played their part in the group or society to which they belonged. What we see, then, is what we should recognise as a modern attitude to human problems.

The greatness of Wagner lies in the fact that he was able to express his ideas in a unique way. The manner in which he expressed himself we can both analyse and appreciate, or (better still) understand without analysing. The part of Wagner's genius that we can appreciate appears in the means of expression that he formulated. We should, however, understand that this is not the whole of his genius. This embraces the selection and examination of the underlying human ideas and their change into music.

It has been shown that artistic excellence depends on hard work. No man ever worked harder than Wagner. By the time he was compelled to flee from Dresden *Rienzi* (1842), *The Flying Dutchman* (1843), and *Tannhäuser* (1845) had been produced. As one work followed another so did the shape of a new kind of opera begin to show itself : an opera in which there is not, as formerly, division of the work into separate 'numbers', and in which the intertwining of melodic and harmonic ideas both symbolise action and help to maintain a continuous musical flow.

Audiences at first reacted badly. It was tiresome not to know when a song had finished and when one could applaud a favourite singer. It was also perplexing not to know what was recitative and what was aria.

During the second half of the nineteenth century Wagner was the most talked-of musician in Europe. He was then the most modern of modern composers. He lived in Switzerland for more than ten years until he could have permission once again to return to Germany. He worked at the four operas that together make the cycle known as *The Nibelung's Ring*. The four operas were *The Rhinegold*, *The Valkyrie*, *Siegfried* (the hero of the whole cycle), and *The Twilight of the Gods*.

These operas were founded on ancient Scandinavian myths that had made their way into the folk-literature of medieval Germany. The story of Siegfried is of a man of great powers who is destroyed partly by the faults in his own nature, partly by the corrupt and hostile forces of the world. *The Ring*, with its vast assembly of characters, was envisaged as a great moral drama – akin to the old 'moralities' – and was designed to be performed as a whole during a period of four days.

It was many years before Wagner saw his intention fulfilled. Before this became possible he composed *Tristan and Isolde* (1857–9) and *The Mastersingers of Nürnberg* (1862–7). The former contains some of the most moving love-music ever written. The latter, Wagner's one comedy, gives a lively picture of German life in a provincial city.

At the age of fifty Wagner was fortunate in winning the support and friendship of King Ludwig II of Bavaria. He was invited to live in Munich and plans were drawn up to build a new opera-house in Munich, so that *The Ring* could be performed as Wagner intended that it should. It was not, however, in Munich but in Bayreuth that the theatre of Wagner's dreams was built. After many setbacks this project came to fulfilment in 1876 and in the August of that year the first festival performance of *The Ring* took place. This was a landmark in the history of opera; for the new type of opera that Wagner had worked the whole of his life to achieve was not only shown in its proper form but was also applauded and accepted by the public.

In his last years Wagner completed one more opera, *Parsifal,* in which the Christian ideas already shown in *Tannhäuser* and *Lohengrin* are made the centre of the whole conception. *Parsifal* was performed for the first time in 1882. By describing this work as a 'sacred dramatic festival' and by hoping that it would never be produced in a 'profane' opera-house Wagner went right back to the starting-point of the theatre; that is, the church.

Wagner was a great constructive force in the history of music. He was also a great destructive force. It is not possible to be the one without also being the other. He exercised powerful social influence also – both constructive and destructive. Through the character of his dramatic works he gave to his countrymen a sense of pride and unity. There are those who think that he helped, though unconsciously, to turn national pride into national arrogance. Wagner's ideas were not only given expression through music but also through literature. He wrote a very large number of prose works, both on artistic and political matters.

It is probable that we know more about what Wagner thought than about any other composer. It is, however, what he *did* that is of lasting value. What he did, briefly, was to give a new depth of meaning to music, to fit it to the temperament of modern society. Wagner lived on the threshhold of the greatest revolution in human affairs that the world has ever known. The nature of the revolution is known to each of us – at least in part – for we are living through it. The crisis in human affairs centres not so much on man's intellect, but on his emotions and the way in which these are harnessed. Wagner in his music laid out this side of our nature as no other musician had done.

Once again we return to a central idea – the idea that runs throughout this book. Music springs from and appeals to the emotional side of human nature. If we do not appreciate this, then we are not in any position to 'appreciate' music. There is much else besides : but that music is a language of the emotions is indisputable. This is what Shakespeare meant when he spoke of music, as 'the food of love'. In an essay on Beethoven's overture to *Coriolanus*, Wagner says the same thing in a different way : 'the musicians', he wrote, 'can only express moods, feelings, passions and their opposites. . . .' This is what he set out to do in his music-dramas.

Wagner the composer looked back beyond Mozart, and Gluck, to the first days of opera. He saw that the theory that music and drama should come together on equal terms was the only one that was valid. He understood that Beethoven had opened the book of music so that all could read it. He recognised that the technical developments of the nineteenth century had made it possible for a composer to make use of an infinite range of musical colours and designs. He used whatever was available to the full, and in so doing destroyed the conventions within which timid, narrowly professional musicians were held.

Wagner was guided by ambition. He knew what he wished to achieve and he let nothing stand in his path. At the end of his combative and restless life – in the course of which his selfishness and ruthlessness caused great distress to many people – he could see the culmination of his labours. He was the greatest composer of his time, and one of the greatest composers of all time. That this was so was through the realisation of one idea – the idea that in this book stands as the 'great idea'. This was that music only mattered when it was a part of life itself. Wagner was a Romantic composer, but he did not romanticise. He knew from the legend of Faust that men were corruptible. This is the note that sounds again and again amid the heroics of the music-dramas. That, perhaps, is why he arrived finally at the point in religion : 'What is man that thou art mindful of him.'

Wagner was the end of a great age of music. His works, as we have seen in the first chapter, were also the beginning of a new era in musical expression.

In a terrible moment in the second act of *The Twilight of the Gods*, Brynhilda, who loves Siegfried, believes him to be guilty of deceit and treachery. He swears he is not. Brynhilda does not believe him. The music that expresses this situation is set at the beginning of the chapter.

Music like that was not known before Wagner : but since his day similar melodic and harmonic arrangements at last have become a regular part of our experience. This is the music not of certainty, but of doubt. Perhaps you can see how music does say something about the way in which we live. But each age, and each society, must strive to find the best way to achieve this. When we say each 'age' or each 'society' we must realise that it is the individual who determines finally what is to be done. So Wagner, the artist, commanded the attention of the musical world at one time, and Schoenberg at another. Where does the next 'great idea' come from?

RECOMMENDED BOOKS

CHAPTER

1   David Ewen, *The Complete Book of 20th Century Music*, Prentice Hall, New York, and Blond, London, 1961

ed. Hans Gal, *The Musician's World*, Thames and Hudson, London, 1965

(an interesting selection of letters written by composers of all periods)

Herbert Weinstock, *What Music Is*, Doubleday, New York, 1966 (a general survey, with an invaluable section on modern music)

2   John Gillespie, *Five Centuries of Keyboard Music*, Wadsworth Pub. Co., Inc., Belmont, California, 1965

Rosamund E. M. Harding, *The Pianoforte*, Cambridge University Press, 1933

3   H. C. Robbins Landon, *The Complete Correspondence and London Notebooks of Joseph Haydn*, Barrie and Rockliff, London, 1959

Rosemary Hughes, *Haydn String Quartets*, B.B.C., London, 1966

Christina Stadtlaender, *Joseph Haydn of Eisenstadt*, Dobson, London, 1968

4   ed. Anthony Baines, *Musical Instruments through the Ages*, Faber and Faber, London, 1966

Karl Geiringer, *Musical Instruments: their History in Western Culture*, Allen and Unwin, London, 1943

5   ed. Dom Anselm Hughes, *The New Oxford History of Music* (Vol. II, *Early Medieval Music up to 1300*), O.U.P., London, 1954

Alec Robertson, *Sacred Music*, Max Parrish, London, Chanticleer Press, New York, 1945

6   ed. Hans David and Arthur Mendel, *The Bach Reader*, Norton, New York, J. M. Dent, London, 1945/1967

J. A. Fuller-Maitland, *The '48', Bach's Wohltemperirtes Clavier*, 2 vol. O.U.P., London, 1925

7   Bence Szabolcsi, *The History of Melody*, Barrie and Rockliff, London, 1966

8   Donald Grout, *A Short History of Opera*, Columbia University Press, New York, and O.U.P., London (revised ed. 2 vol.) 1966

[G.] Kobbé, *Complete Opera Book*, ed. and revised by the Earl of Harewood, Putnam, London and New York, 1958

Michael F. Robinson, *Opera before Mozart*, Hutchinson, London, 1966

9   Percy M. Young, *The Choral Tradition*, Hutchinson, London, Norton, New York (revised ed.) 1967

10   *Dictionary of Modern Ballet*, Tudor, New York, Methuen, London, 1959

ed. David Drew, *The Decca Book of Ballet*, Frederick Muller, London, 1958

J. Gregory, *Understanding Ballet*, Oldbourne Press, London, Burns and MacEachern, New York, 1965

F. Reyna, *Concise History of the Ballet*, Thames and Hudson, London, Grosset, New York, 1965

11   Grout and Robinson as under 8 above

E.McA. Gagey, *Ballad Opera*, Columbia University Press, New York, 1937

12   Edward Dent, *Opera*, Penguin Books, London, 1940/1949
      Richard Wagner, *My Life* (only to 1848), Constable,
         London, 1911

An invaluable one-volume work of reference : *The International
Cyclopedia of Music and Musicians*, ed. by Oscar Thompson
and others, Dodd, Mead & Co., Inc., New York, J. M. Dent,
London, many editions. Also recommended for general reading :
F. Dorian, *The History of Music in Performance*, Norton,
New York, 1942.

RECOMMENDED RECORDINGS

(stereo recordings shown in brackets)

203

Richard Strauss
    Concertos No. 1 in E flat, Op. 11, and No. 2 in
    E flat, horn and orch.
    Columbia – 33CX 1491
5 Gregorian Chant
    Mass for Christmas Day
    Archive – APM 14153 (SAPM 198153)
    Mass for Easter Sunday
    Archive – APM 14017
6 Johann Sebastian Bach
    Das Wohltemperirte Klavier ('48' Preludes and
    Fugues) Nos. 1–24, played on harpsichord
    Deutsche Grammophon – LPM 18844–5 (SLPM
    13844–5)
    played on clavichord
    Archive – APM 14311–2 (SAPM 198311–2)
    played on pianoforte
    H.M.V. – HQM 1042–3 (HAS 1042–3)
7 Zoltán Kodály
    Háry János (with Stravinsky, *Petrouchka*)
    C.B.S. – BRG 72362 (SBRG 72362)
8 Giulio Caccini and Jacopo Peri
    Songs
    H.M.V. – 1847
  Claudio Monteverdi
    L'Incoronazione di Popœa
    H.M.V. – AN 126–7 (SAN 126–7)
9 George Frideric Handel
    Messiah
    Philips – AL 3584–6 (SAL 3584–6)
  Felix Mendelssohn
    Elijah
    Vox – VBX 208 (SVBX 5208)

Edward Elgar
The Dream of Gerontius
H.M.V. – ALP 2101–2 (ASD 648–9)
10 Jean Rameau
Les Indes galantes (Suite)
Vox – DL 1070 (STDL50 1070)
Igor Stravinsky
L'oiseau de feu
H.M.V. – ALP 2112 (ASD 654)
11 Giovanni Pergolesi
La serva padrona
Delyse – ECB 3178 (DS 6078)
12 Albert Lortzing
Undine (excerpts)
Telefunken – GMA 59
Czar and Zimmermann (excerpts)
Decca – LXT 6039 (SXL 6039)
Richard Wagner
Tannhäuser (excerpts)
H.M.V. – ALP 2005 (ASD 550)
Die Walküre (excerpts)
R.C.A. Victor – RB 6558 (SB 6558)
Parsifal (excerpts)
Philips – GL 5821 (SGL 5821)

INDEX